MISSION VEGAN

ALSO BY DANNY BOWIEN
*The Mission Chinese Food
Cookbook*

MISSION VEGAN

WILDLY DELICIOUS FOOD FOR EVERYONE

DANNY BOWIEN

WITH JJ GOODE

An Imprint of HarperCollinsPublishers

CONTENTS

FOREWORD

BY KIM HASTREITER

I'll never forget the night I first met Danny Bowien. The year was 2011 and I was in San Francisco with my crazy bestie Joey Arias to perform with my other brilliant friend Thomas Lauderdale's band Pink Martini. For fun, Thomas had invited Joey to sing and me to play the triangle and cymbals as guest performers with the band for a few nights at the Symphony Hall there. None of us were from San Francisco, but I had some great friends there who knew everything and everybody from the underground up and steered us to the best newest, most genius stuff to do and see while we were in town. As usual, I became the "tour guide" bossing my posse around about what we should do, buy, eat, and see. Casing out the alternative city culture as soon as I arrived, I immediately discovered that at that moment in time, San Francisco seemed to be nurturing a whole fresh youth cultural movement that was centered around FOOD.

As a self-described cultural anthropologist, seeing this new generation latching onto food as culture in this town where the queen mother–legend of New American Cuisine—the visionary Alice Waters—had opened Chez Panisse in 1971 made sense to me. Waters had changed *everything* with Chez Panisse. Her powerful philosophy of serving only ethically and locally sourced food cooked simply was new and began a seismic change in American cuisine, eventually putting the United States on the global culinary map. News of her then-radical ideas spread, turning San Francisco in the seventies into a culinary mecca for food makers and lovers everywhere. And now, forty years later, new generations seemed to be picking up the baton and continuing to shake things up once again.

As soon as I arrived in town, the very first thing I was emphatically instructed to do with my big motley crew was to head down to Mission Street and wait in line for a table at an innocuous, generic-looking, old, beaten-up Chinese restaurant there called Lung Shan, where some young punk-y kids had supposedly taken over the kitchen guerilla-style a few nights a week and were serving a super radical and creative menu (alongside the OG Chinese takeout fare). All my Frisco friends were talking about this. The buzz was BIG. The lines were LONG. The food was RAD. The idea was NEW. The prices were DEMOCRATIC. The ingredients were ETHICAL. And the chef/cofounder (Danny Bowien) was COLORFUL, COOL, and TALENTED. Oh, and he was supposed to be really really NICE, too.

The wait was quite a while, so our whole Pink Martini crew happily joined the party taking place on the sidewalk with the other hungry festive local culture vultures outside waiting to get in. When we finally got our table, I discovered Danny was a fan of *Paper* (the magazine I used to make back then). He took the time to give us a giant warm welcome in the middle of his chaotic and overwhelming night. The place was pumping, Danny was racing around like an athlete, and I loved him immediately. We ordered everything on the menu. And with every dish delivery, he checked in with us like an eager puppy to see how we liked it all. Of course, his kung pao pastrami was the star of the night for everybody. It kind of summed up Mission Chinese Food's rebel attitude to me and how this new generation of subversive kids were pushing boundaries with their new medium. They were turning it all upside down, experimenting with OG cultural dishes while respecting the provenance, ethics, and heritage of San Francisco's early "eat-local" mavericks like Ms. Waters.

Now, I am not a part of the culinary world or a food critic. I am a culture person. I've spent my whole life and career chasing creative subcultural movements—and the subversive energy of dinner that night eleven years ago really struck a chord with me. After stuffing ourselves to the gills, I left Mission Chinese that night with the strong feeling in my gut that something new *culturally* was going on with these new creatives coming up in this town. Danny was the kind of rebel kid that years before (if he'd been in my generation) would've channeled that energy into making art, starting a band in his garage, or shooting Super 8 movies underground. As I sniffed around San Francisco that trip, I began to notice more and more very cool young folks who were making culture around food—growing it, cooking it, butchering it, reinventing it, fusing it, and most important, building communities around it. I was so inspired by this new young San Francisco food scene that I decided then and there that I needed to create a special food issue of *Paper*. Danny Bowien was the one who excited me the most that trip, so I crammed in a few more visits before I left town and by the time I returned home, I'd made a new friend. As I pulled my food issue together six months later, I got word that Danny had rented a little basement spot on Orchard Street to open a Mission in NYC. I was ecstatic! So of course he became part of my issue, front and center.

From the moment my issue came out and Danny moved to NYC, I watched his journey become a saga. As years passed, Mission opened and closed on Orchard Street, reopened in Chinatown, opened in Bushwick, closed in Chinatown. He hustled his ass off, as we New Yorkers tend to do. But all throughout his journey, the one consistent thing that Danny brought to my city was a sense of community. And throughout it all, I saw clearly that my friend Danny was happiest when he was feeding this community.

Mission Chinese became my canteen. I met so many people and made so many friends there over the years. Danny introduced me to his posse of young friends there, and of course I'd drag my family of OGs to Mission often so he met my old friends there. Our friends then met each other and young and older generations of like-minded creative New Yorkers got all mixed up. So much love in that place. Friends got married. Friends got divorced. Friends got famous, friends had babies, friends fell in love, friends went into rehab, friends even died. There are so many stories. Like the time Danny cooked for twenty-five of us at Mission after the huge women's march before the catastrophe of Donald Trump's presidency began. Or the first birthday party at Mission Chinese of Danny and Youngmi's beautiful son, Mino, who was dressed in traditional Korean gowns. I remember the day well, especially the huge platters of food they served from neighborhood places like Katz's Deli and Russ & Daughters. Danny loved those kinds of legendary old-school New York spots. He was always excited to turn me on to somewhere he loved. Like the time he took me to eat my first burger at Peter Luger (with no reservation and no wait) or schlepped with me for the first time to Barney Greengrass for matzoh brei or to some insane sushi place on the Upper East Side or to his favorite old-school Ballato's for spaghetti and meatballs on Houston Street. And everywhere he went he'd bring bags of his mapo tofu or hotter than hell chicken wings as a treat for the staff at whatever restaurant he was eating at. Of course, Danny was beloved and treated so well everywhere. I remember Danny hosting a Pink Martini practice once during Mission Chinese off hours for a gaggle of my friends who were immigrants from all over the world. It was at the beginning of the Trump years and so I invited lots of my immigrant friends to perform the song "America" from *West Side Story* at Brooklyn Academy of Music that night. Danny joined us onstage!

Which brings me to Danny's generosity. Danny is much more comfortable giving than receiving. He loved to give his food to people. He'd always drop food over if I was sick or bring tons of his food to parties I might throw. He knew I couldn't eat spicy food, so Danny cooked everything on the menu special for me: no chilies. Our dear late friend Jim Walrod hated any kind of vegetables, so Danny made all his greatest hits for Jim with no veggies.

Many of the kids downtown were vegan so Danny began to offer, among other things, vegan mapo tofu, which became a big hit. Danny, who kept his killer lamb, ribs, beef, broccoli, and pastrami on the menu, started adding lots more vegan dishes so the vegan kids would be able to eat there, too. It was a challenge for him, I think, but he got into it big-time, aiming to create innovative vegan dishes that nonvegans would love too. Danny made a vegan kabocha congee that I flipped for. It was the most divine-tasting thing and I became addicted to it. I ate so much of it he now calls it Kim's Kabocha Congee on the menu. It's even in this book, so I urge you to make it as its high on the list of my favorite foods in the world.

Looking at this beautiful new book you hold in your hands, some might think that Danny is now a vegan and Mission Chinese Food is a vegan restaurant. Nope. This book is just a facet of the complex and wonderful Danny Bowien. It is more about his democratic nature and generosity of spirit that makes him want to please and include everyone who comes by his restaurant, whether meat eaters or not. Until recently, vegans often have had a difficult time finding amazing, innovative, and delicious plant-based food that they could dine on with any of their friends, whether vegan or not. Danny made this vision happen. And people loved it. But Danny tells his own story best in his own words. It's a great story that explains how and why he became who he is. Once you read this you will understand this is more than just another cookbook. It's a gift to us all from Danny.

INTRODUCTION

Danny as a senior
on the way to school in 2000

I was nineteen when I left Oklahoma to move to San Francisco. I got off the plane, jumped on a bus, and before I'd even seen my new apartment, I was eating kimchi for the first time in my life.

On my two-block walk from the bus stop to my apartment, I spotted Muguboka, a frill-free Korean restaurant on Balboa Street, and wandered in with my bags. It took them a few moments, but the people who ran Muguboka quickly worked out that the Korean-looking kid with long emo-rocker hair and a studded white belt didn't speak a word of Korean and had never eaten Korean food.

It's not that there weren't any Korean restaurants back home in Oklahoma City. I just wasn't particularly interested in finding them. Partly because I was happy eating fried chicken at Eischen's, spicy tuna rolls at Sushi Neko, bún bò Huế at Phở Cường (which used to be a Long John Silver's), and shrimp fajitas at Chelino's, which came on a sizzling platter, a feature I'd eventually borrow and use at every restaurant I've ever opened, because it embodies the loud, head-turning fun I aspired to in everything I make. But also partly because I wanted to keep my parents comfortable. I thought that maybe taking their adopted son to eat the food of his ancestral homeland, where I'd lived for all of three months as an infant, had the potential to be meaningful and therefore possibly kind of awkward.

THAT FIRST TIME AT MUGUBOKA, I was full of the unbridled optimism my move to San Francisco had stirred in me. On paper, I had moved here to go to culinary school. I was a Food Network kid. My heroes were Emeril and Bobby, and after my mom died, my band broke up, and I (barely) graduated high school, I followed a friend to the Bay. The moment I arrived, everything felt possible, for all the reasons most kids get pumped to be on their own. And also because I was finally free of some of the burdens of my life in Oklahoma—especially the ever-present "What's *your* deal?" question that came when people saw Korean me next to my white parents.

In that sense, stepping into Muguboka felt familiar. Unfamiliar was what or how to order, so I asked them to feed me, and they did, beginning with half a dozen small plates set on my table. There were blanched bean sprouts dressed with sesame oil, sweet slabs of lotus root, a tangle of dark green seaweed, and red-tinged squares of cabbage. By the time they brought out the spicy pork, broiled mackerel, and kimchi stew that they'd picked for me, I'd emptied most of the little dishes, just like I used to demolish the chips and queso at Chelino's before my fajitas came. On my next visit a few days later, I naively tried to order the little dishes with some rice, only to be informed that these were banchan—the assortment came with every meal, not on their own.

I felt strange when that first meal ended. Not because I had flashes of some alternate life where I was never put up for adoption and was instead raised on sujebi and doenjang-guk. It may have been the sense that even though the flavors were mostly unfamiliar, they all immediately made sense to me. I liked *everything*. What did that mean?

Muguboka became my neighborhood restaurant. It was the first time I had found a place where I wasn't just another customer, where I was cared for. It was also the first time I felt like a member of a Korean family. The language barrier meant we never moved beyond small talk, but I felt their affection. They were like aunts and I was the kid at the family barbecue, with cheeks to be pinched. I'd show up on my way to class, holding my student-chef whites, and they'd tell me how cute I was, urge me to try out for some K-Pop version of *American Idol*, and send me off to school with a Styrofoam clamshell full of banchan and a container of hot rice.

After graduating culinary school, a program that was supposed to take eight months but took me something like three years, I bopped around various kitchens, where I learned to make sushi rice and slice hamachi before I wound up at Farina in the Mission. It was funny. Here I was, someone whose previous experiences with Italian food were bowls of alfredo at Olive Garden and shrimp scampi at Red Lobster, cooking under the tutelage of an uncompromising Ligurian. The chef, Paolo Laboa, showed me how to make fresh pasta, octopus terrines, and the pesto his grandma's grandma's grandma once made. He was the reason for my first brush with fame—in 2008, he took me to the World Pesto Championship in Genoa. I had assumed I'd just be assisting Paolo, but then I somehow found myself among the competitors, me and a hundred others, most of them from Liguria, clutching olivewood pestles and marble mortars, and Paolo too far away to handhold. As an Asian American, I made a real splash even before they announced the winner. The next day, I took an early jet-lagged walk in Genoa and saw front-page headlines in every local newspaper screaming that a Korean chef from California had won. It was crazy.

You might've already heard what happened next. I met Anthony Myint, who had launched Mission Street Food, first as a food cart then eventually as a pop-up that operated out of a nondescript Cantonese restaurant on Mission Street called Lung Shan. He'd invited an array of chef collaborators to cook inventive dinners that they could never have made at the white tablecloth restaurants where they trained. He let me pitch in.

Not long after, on a flight home from my first trip to Korea, where I'd just gotten married, I got an email from Anthony. He was moving on, he wanted me to take over, and he offered to help me make our Sichuan night pop-up at Lung Shan permanent.

Winning the World Pesto Championship in 2008

At the time, my nights-off obsession was eating Chinese with Anthony, my friend and fellow cook Brandon Jew, and whoever else we could convince to join us in order to increase the amount of food it would be reasonable to order. Poring through my memories of those dinners and a pile of Brandon's cookbooks, including Fuchsia Dunlop's *Land of Plenty* and Iron Chef Chen Kenichi's *Knockout Chinese*, produced Mission Chinese Food, which was Chinese food in the same way that what Anthony and friends served on Lung Shan's wobbly tables was street food.

When diners came in, they were handed two menus: Lung Shan's wide-ranging, fold-out menu of Cantonese dishes and a single page listing the dishes I'd come up with. There were wings prepared in the style of the Chongqing chicken at Z & Y Restaurant in Chinatown. There was Taiwanese-style eggplant, for which I borrowed a brine-fry-and-blanch technique from Paolo at Farina. There was salt cod fried rice that tasted, inexplicably and in the best way, like Taco Bell. My sense of the borders between cuisines was blurred then, and I guess they still kind of are.

Recipe testing at Mission in January 2020

The food spawned devoted fans, fervent detractors, and a lot of people eager to see what the fuss was about. The legend of the Oklahoma-raised Korean adoptee who had won the pesto championship and now made kung pao pastrami was born. Just as a Korean kid with two white parents had people scratching their heads back home, my peculiar, inscrutable identity had everyone scratching their heads now. When your existence makes people feel uncomfortable, you work very hard to make them feel better. That's what I did back in Oklahoma, and that's what I did now: Let's eat.

At the start of 2020, I was deep into a new cookbook that reflected how the food at the restaurant had changed over its decade in existence. Since the first iteration of Mission opened, I had married, become a father, got sober, and got divorced, in more or less that order. I'd succeeded spectacularly and, in many ways, failed spectacularly, too. A lot had changed, including my cooking. I was growing up.

I began experimenting with cooking vegan food for myself and others, though I have never been strict enough about what I eat to claim the "vegan" title. When I was a young chef, I was all about destroying my body with beef and booze—now I was craving food that left me feeling good. I started enjoying the challenge of making food taste good and feel satisfying without leaning on cured pork, oyster sauce, and lamb ribs. Vegan food also felt more inclusive. I'd often hear friends say, "Man, I wish I could come to Mission, but I don't eat meat," and I would tell them that half of the menu was actually vegan. We just didn't make a big deal about it and most people didn't really notice. Everyone can eat vegan food, and if it tastes awesome, everyone will.

While the cookbook started as a vegan greatest hits record, for vegans and non-vegans alike, it took another turn when the world came to a halt. My days went from cooking in the restaurant to fretting over whether it was safe to serve food at all and pondering whether a Korean adoptee raised in Oklahoma should even be cooking Chinese food in the first place. I started mulling a question that applied to my businesses and the cookbook and my entire life: What happens now?

That's when I thought of that first meal at Muguboka and the journey I've been on since. I thought of my first trip to Korea for my wedding to Youngmi, who was born in Cheonan, Korea, and, unlike me, speaks Korean and feels connected to the culture of her Korean mother. While it wasn't exactly a homecoming—I felt as out of place there as I have almost everywhere else—the trip was a joyful education. It was there, after seeing me gawping at the Noryangjin Fish Market and eating several bowls of ice-cold naengmyeon in quick succession, that Youngmi said, "You should cook Korean food, just do it." While I had brashly thrown myself into Chinese cooking and otherwise operated on the principle of "Why not?" this somehow felt off-limits.

The answer was complicated. Throughout my life, people have asked me whether I'd ever want to meet my real parents. The response that gave people the tidy, sweet story I knew they wanted was to explain that my adopted parents are my real parents. My shrugging response to Youngmi's proposition all those years ago was similar. It was way easier to embrace my unconventional culinary narrative, which treated my Korean-ness, whatever that was, as incidental and disposable. Misdirection was my way of saying to curious onlookers that that part of my story was none of their business.

I ALSO THOUGHT ABOUT MY second trip to Korea, years later, when I had an incredible full-circle experience, traveling there with Emeril Lagasse, the TV chef who had BAMed me into wanting to cook in the first place. We cooked with Jeong Kwan, a Buddhist nun, master of vegan Korean temple food, and chef with no restaurant. She didn't aspire to fame or fortune. The big showstoppers I specialized in felt silly next to her food, which delivered the emotional impact and wow factor I chased in just a sliver of kimchi. Looking back, I realize that this moment broke down a big wall for me about vegan food. Jeong Kwan's food wasn't about food that lacked anything. It was just profound and incredibly delicious cooking.

Emeril and I also stumbled across a Mission Chinese Food copycat in Seoul. When the show's producers had us go there, I spotted the owner looking kind of terrified, as if he'd been caught in the act. But I wasn't mad. I was thrilled. Someone liked me. In Korea. This was meaningful in a way that none of the fanfare around Mission had ever been. It got me thinking: Maybe I could actually be accepted for who I'd become.

A year later, while filming *The Mind of a Chef*, I had my lightbulb moment. For one episode, I got the chance to cook for the legendary chef Yu Bo in Chengdu. I made him mapo tofu, a classic Sichuan dish, but with lamb instead of pork. Changing the dish was one part respect and one part hedge—it's scary to make a dish that exists, so I made something that didn't. When Yu Bo pronounced it legit, the affirmation gave me a new

Learning about doubanjiang with Chef Yu Bo

kind of confidence in myself. I felt a shift. What if I did try to cook Korean food one day? Why not?

Back in New York, I began spending my nights off eating sundubu-jjigae in Koreatown and icy-cold buckwheat noodles in Flushing, just like I'd been haunting City View for dim sum and R&G Lounge for golden fried rice back in San Francisco before opening Mission. I had started dabbling in some Korean flavors and ingredients at home and at the restaurants, yet for years, my life was too chaotic to explore something new. But shutting one restaurant and temporarily closing another gave me time to pause.

When we reopened in the summer of 2020, the menu at Mission started changing. I was making my interpretation of Korean food, pulling from my memories and pantry and preferences to make what I think is really good to eat. I cooked by intuition to make the mung bean pancakes and kimchi dumplings I'd had at street markets in Seoul, same as I did when I started making kung pao and tingly lamb soup.

Mission today is not a vegan restaurant nor is it a Korean one. It's a restaurant that continues to evolve, as it always has. While my first book documented a journey I'd already taken, this book is about embarking on a new adventure.

Eating and cooking has long been my way of exploring who I am. My identity, like the food I make, is constantly evolving. Which is why in this book, you'll find pasta pomodoro in the same chapter as chewy Korean buckwheat noodles topped with dragon fruit ice, tofu skin in the style of cumin lamb, and green tea noodles that taste like Vietnamese phở.

Because the way I cook often reflects where I'm at on this journey, a good portion of the recipes in these pages are inspired by Korean food and the Korean meal. Yet the recipes themselves, like those in my last book, reflect my restless mind, my various preferences and quirks. I might not be qualified to coach you through making proper versions of Korean classics, but I do love what I've come up with and I like sharing what I love.

The coolest thing about this book is that the recipes are way more straightforward than those in my first one. And, if you ask me, they often best the more complicated stuff. Take mapo tofu. The version in my previous book took three days. The vegan one here? It takes an hour, and tastes even better.

Anyone can cook from this book, skilled or not, vegan or not. Because what's the point of having a party if your friends can't all go?

At Muguboka Restaurant in San Francisco

KIMCHI

KIMCHI TIPS

In Korea, I didn't see many kimchi makers breaking out the scale or measuring cups, but that's because they've been making it so long that they can operate by feel. They know by instinct how much salt will kill bad bacteria and draw out enough liquid from vegetables to create a brine that encourages good ones.

Until you get there, though, precision is important. That's why when it really matters, I've provided the weights rather than volumes, so please use a cheapo digital kitchen scale and stick to these weights. That way, your early forays into lacto-fermentation will be stress-free.

The process for each ferment in this book is essentially the same. You toss vegetables with salt, so they soften and release liquid. You add seasonings. Then you add the mixture to clean glass jars with tight-fitting lids. Often, you want to give the mixture a firm press to force out any air bubbles and to ensure the liquid brine fully submerges the stuff you mean to ferment. For insurance, I advise adding plastic wrap pressed against the surface of the brine and a weight to prevent any potential bobbing to the surface. That weight could be a small jar or ramekin (anything that fits inside the mouth of the larger jar) or a resealable bag filled with water, double-bagged so it doesn't leak.

From there, you just set the jar out at room temperature (65°F to 70°F is the sweet spot, 60°F to 75°F is just fine). There's some leeway on either end of that spectrum, which will affect the speed at which it ferments (hotter = quicker, cooler = slower). I like to taste it at various stages, before I add the mixture to the jar and every day or so, just to get a sense of how it changes. As time passes, the saltiness will mellow and the ferment will get more sour, funky, and complex.

Each recipe gives a suggested range of time for fermentation, but the important thing is to ferment to your liking. I tend to enjoy sturdy vegetables fermented longer than more delicate ones. Once they're fermented to your liking, transfer them to the fridge, where they'll keep for 4 to 6 weeks (and likely longer). They'll continue fermenting, just much more slowly.

If you follow my instructions, you won't have to worry about spoilage, but do note that in the rare case that you spot any mold (anything fuzzy or a film that's a color other than white), be safe, dump it, and start over. White film on the surface of the brine is likely kahm yeast. It's not dangerous, but you should carefully skim it off, because it can contribute off-flavors.

Note: *The only salt to avoid when making kimchi is iodized salt, because the iodine content can inhibit fermentation. I often use kosher salt, but Korean markets sell coarse sea salt that's used specifically for kimchi making.*

Because salts with different crystal size actually give you different amounts of salt per tablespoon, I suggest you use Diamond Crystal kosher salt for these kimchi, because that's what I used. I've also provided weights, so you can use another type of salt, if you want.

Go-To Cabbage Kimchi (see page 14)

WATERMELON KIMCHI

MAKES ABOUT 2 QUARTS

Watermelon and kimchi might sound like unlikely partners, but they're so not. One of my favorite styles of mul-naengmyeon, cold chewy buckwheat noodles in cold broth, comes with both kimchi and a slice of watermelon on the side. (There's also a style of bibim-naengmyeon where the same buckwheat noodles are dressed and served inside a halved watermelon!) When I decided to try giving watermelon itself the kimchi treatment, I was thinking about the interplay of crunchy, tangy, and spicy with crisp, sweet, and juicy, about my affection for vinegar-pickled watermelon rind popular in the American South, and about my fascination with the pickled watermelon wedges in the Russian markets in Brighton Beach.

The result is really exciting—the rind is crunchy and effervescent, and the flesh turns savory and tart with this roasted-red-pepper texture.

Note: The weights here are important. See why on page 2.

2½ pounds seedless watermelon, unpeeled, cut into small, 1-inch-thick wedges

37 grams (¼ cup) Diamond Crystal kosher salt

7½ ounces coarsely grated white onion

6½ ounces coarsely grated peeled Korean radish, daikon, or red radish

5 tablespoons gochugaru (Korean chili flakes)

PUT the watermelon and salt in a large mixing bowl and toss, gently so you don't break the wedges, to coat well. Let it hang out for 10 minutes, so the salt draws some liquid from the melon.

IN a medium mixing bowl, combine the onion, radish, and gochugaru and mix well. Add the mixture to the bowl with the watermelon and toss gently but well, firmly packing the paste onto the watermelon wedges to make sure that the chili mixture coats the flesh, rind, and peel.

TRANSFER to a clean wide-mouthed 2-quart glass jar, being careful not to break the wedges. If there's anything left in the bowl, scrape it into the container. Use a spoon to push down on the mixture so the liquid rises to submerge or nearly submerge the watermelon. Cover with plastic wrap, pressing it against the surface of the mixture. Cover tightly with a lid and let it ferment at room temperature (see page 2) until it sours slightly, 4 to 5 days, burping the container after 2 days.

AFTER it's fermented to your liking, store it in the fridge for up to 6 weeks.

PINEAPPLE KIMCHI

MAKES ABOUT 2 QUARTS

Like most kids, I was into pineapple growing up, forking it from those little fruit cups with the foil lids and the neon red cherry inside, but I had never eaten the fresh fruit until one Thanksgiving when my uncle Bud brought a couple over. For some reason, even though my dad cut them up and set them out, no one had any. Except me. I ate both. I savored every bite—and I was sick for days after.

Despite that, I'm crazy about pineapple now. So when the kitchen at Mission was messing around with kimchi a while back, I thought, Why not? I'm definitely not the first person to ferment the fruit. After all, there's the Mexican drink tepache. There's pineapple vinegar in the Philippines. And there's the highbrow restaurant I worked at years ago where we fermented it to serve with oysters. Turns out, kimchi is another great way to explore pineapple's savory side, bumping up its acidity and balancing its remaining sweetness with salt and heat. It's especially delicious in fried rice (page 166).

Note: The weights here are important. See why on page 2.

1½ pounds peeled, cored, and cubed (1-inch) ripe pineapple

28 grams (3 tablespoons plus 1 teaspoon) Diamond Crystal kosher salt

17 ounces coarsely grated white onion

11 ounces coarsely grated Korean radish or daikon

5 tablespoons gochugaru (Korean chili flakes)

PUT the pineapple in a large mixing bowl, sprinkle on the salt, and toss well. Let stand until the pineapple starts to give up some liquid, about 10 minutes. Add the onion, radish, and gochugaru and stir well.

TRANSFER to a clean 2-quart glass jar. Use a spoon to push down on the mixture so the liquid rises to submerge or nearly submerge the pineapple. Cover with plastic wrap, pressing it against the surface of the mixture, then add a small weight. Cover tightly with a lid and let it ferment at room temperature (see page 2) until it sours slightly, 2 to 4 days, burping the container after 3 days.

AFTER it's fermented to your liking, store it in the fridge for up to 6 weeks.

HABANERO KIMCHI

MAKES ABOUT 1½ QUARTS

This one is (sort of) a white kimchi, the array of Korean ferments made without the gochugaru that gives many other kimchi varieties their red color and heat. White kimchi is typically mild, but here I add my favorite fresh chili, the fiery habanero. Giving them a quick char over an open flame adds a subtle smokiness to their already incredible flavor, so fruity and floral and unlike any other chili I've ever had. (Except maybe for their relative the Scotch bonnet, which also works great here.)

Note: The weights here are important. See why on page 2.

30 ounces Napa cabbage, base trimmed of any blemished parts

25 grams (3 tablespoons) Diamond Crystal kosher salt

1½ tablespoons shio koji (creamy white koji)

3 habanero chilies, stemmed

21 ounces trimmed Korean radish or daikon, cut into thin half-moon slices

1½ tablespoons finely chopped garlic

1½ tablespoons grated ginger

QUARTER the cabbage, cut each quarter lengthwise into thirds, then slice it all crosswise into 1-inch pieces. Combine the cabbage, salt, and koji in a large mixing bowl and toss well to evenly coat. Let it hang out for about 15 minutes, until the cabbage has softened and reduced in volume by about a quarter.

MEANWHILE, work one at a time to char the habaneros over an open gas flame, holding them with tongs and turning as they blister and blacken. It'll take a minute or so per chili. When they're done, halve them, scrape out and discard the seeds, and give them a rough chop. Let them cool completely. Add the habaneros, radishes, garlic, and ginger to the cabbage and toss well.

TRANSFER to a clean 2-quart glass jar. Use a spoon to push down on the mixture so the liquid rises to submerge or nearly submerge the vegetables. Cover with plastic wrap, pressing it against the surface of the mixture, then add a small weight. Cover tightly with a lid and let it ferment at room temperature (see page 2) until it sours slightly, 4 to 7 days, burping the container after 3 days.

AFTER it's fermented to your liking, store it in the fridge for up to 6 weeks.

STUFFED CUCUMBER KIMCHI

MAKES 6

This kimchi is exceptional during summer months, when cucumbers are at their peak. Nowadays, cucumbers are available all the time, so you can make this cool stuffed kimchi anytime. It's essentially cucumbers briefly salted, then crammed with the mixture of vegetables, aromatics, and chili flakes you'll recognize in other red kimchi. Serve some right after you make it, when it's fresh and bright and crunchy, and let the rest ferment on the counter so it sours and softens slightly.

2 pounds large kirby cucumbers (about 6)

13 grams (1 tablespoon plus 1½ teaspoons) Diamond Crystal kosher salt

1 cup thinly sliced garlic chives

1 cup thin half-moon slices white onion

1 cup thin carrot matchsticks

¼ cup gochugaru (Korean chili flakes)

3 tablespoons shio koji (creamy white koji)

2 tablespoons finely chopped garlic

2 tablespoons finely chopped ginger

2 tablespoons agave syrup

2 tablespoons toasted sesame seeds

CUT each cucumber *almost* in half lengthwise, stopping an inch or so from the end, then rotate them and make a similar cut to almost but not quite quarter them, again stopping an inch from the end. Put the cucumbers in a large mixing bowl and rub them, inside and out, with the salt, being careful not to break them. Let them hang out for 10 minutes so the salt draws some of the liquid out of the cucumbers.

IN a medium mixing bowl, combine the garlic chives, onion, carrot, gochugaru, shio koji, garlic, ginger, agave syrup, and sesame seeds and stir really well. Drain the cucumbers and give them a quick rinse under cold water, then briefly shake dry. Carefully open the cucumbers, stuff them with some of the mixture, and rub some of the mixture onto the outsides. Pack the cucumbers and the rest of the chili mixture into a clean 1-gallon jar or 2-quart rectangular container, finishing with some of the chili mixture on top.

COVER with plastic wrap, pressing it against the surface of the mixture, then add a small weight. Cover tightly with a lid and let it ferment at room temperature (see page 2) until it sours slightly, 4 to 7 days, burping the container after 3 days.

AFTER it's fermented to your liking, store it in the fridge for up to 2 weeks. Serve the cucumbers whole or snipped into 1-inch pieces.

RADISH WATER KIMCHI

MAKES ABOUT 4 QUARTS

This is my riff on a subcategory of kimchi called mul kimchi, specifically a type within that category called dongchimi, made with radish and traditionally eaten during Korea's cold winters. *Mul* means "water," and the kimchi is made with a brine that becomes a major part of the eating experience, to be spooned up like a cold, tangy, slightly sweet broth with champagne-like bubbles.

There's often a little heat from fresh green chilies, though never, ever from canned pickled jalapeños. Well, never except for now.

Note: The weights here are important. See why on page 2.

One 3- to 4-inch square dasima or dashi kombu

48 grams (¼ cup plus 1 tablespoon) Diamond Crystal kosher salt

2 pounds Korean radish or daikon

3 ounces thinly sliced scallions (1 cup)

One 11-ounce can pickled jalapeños, drained

4 ounces Korean plum extract or ginger kombucha (½ cup)

15 ounces Asian pear (1 medium) or Bosc pears (2 medium), quartered, cored, and thinly sliced lengthwise

9½ ounces white or yellow onion (1 medium), sliced into thin half-moons

½ ounce ginger (1-inch knob), peeled and thinly sliced with the grain

SOAK the dasima in 2 quarts cold water for 30 minutes. Discard the dasima, reserving the liquid. Add 2 tablespoons plus 1 teaspoon of the salt to the liquid and stir until it dissolves.

WHILE the dasima soaks, scrape off any discolored or bruised bits of the radish with a knife. Cut the radish into ¼-inch-thick rounds, then cut the rounds into matchsticks. Toss the radishes with the remaining 2 tablespoons plus 1 teaspoon salt. Mix well and massage, then let the mixture hang out for 20 minutes, so the salt draws some liquid from the radishes. Add the scallions, jalapeños, plum extract, pear, onion, and ginger and stir well.

TRANSFER to a clean 1-gallon (or two 2-quart) glass jars. Pour the dasima-infused water into the jar to submerge the solids. Cover with plastic wrap, pressing it against the surface of the mixture, then add a small weight. Cover tightly with a lid and let it ferment at room temperature (see page 2) until it gives off tiny bubbles resembling champagne, 4 to 7 days, burping the container after 3 days.

AFTER it's fermented to your liking, store it in the fridge for up to 4 weeks.

GO-TO CABBAGE KIMCHI

MAKES ABOUT 2 QUARTS

When my cooking took a Korean turn, we started to send diners at Mission little bowls of this kimchi as a starter. I was proud of it, my first go at vegan kimchi, and it took only eight or nine tries to get the balance of salt, heat, and tang I was after. The kimchi ferments for a few days at room temperature before it's ready, though keep in mind the process continues, slowly, in the fridge. If you can resist eating it all, in a few months you'll have some left that's extra tangy and a little effervescent, perfect for soups, stews, and, if you're like me, snacking.

Note: The weights here are important. See why on page 2.

One 3-pound Napa cabbage

17 grams (2 tablespoons) Diamond Crystal kosher salt

2 tablespoons glutinous rice flour

2 tablespoons granulated sugar

8 ounces yellow or white onion (1 medium), roughly chopped

1½ ounces ginger (4-inch knob), scrubbed and roughly sliced against the grain

½ ounce garlic cloves (5 medium), peeled

8½ ounces gochugaru (Korean chili flakes), about 2 cups

6 tablespoons homemade Mushroom Seasoning Powder (page 231) or 2 ounces store-bought (½ cup)

½ cup sambal oelek

½ cup unseasoned rice vinegar

3 ounces scallions (about 6), trimmed and chopped into 1-inch pieces

REMOVE any bruised leaves from the cabbage and trim any brown stuff from the bottom, but don't cut off the visible core. Halve the cabbage through the core. Cut three 1-inch-deep slits in the bottom of the core of each half. Use your hands to tear each half in half lengthwise (you could use a knife, but I like it better this way). Put the cabbage in a large mixing bowl.

ADD the salt in stages, rubbing it onto the cabbage and between the cabbage leaves until you've used it all. Let the cabbage sit, flipping the quarters every 30 minutes or so, until the leaves have fully wilted and the cabbage has released a lot of liquid, about 4 hours. Drain the cabbage well, discarding the water, and return the cabbage to the bowl.

MEANWHILE, combine the rice flour with 2 cups water in a small saucepan. Set it over high heat, whisking often, until it reaches a boil. Add the sugar, stir well, then pour the mixture into a heatproof bowl to cool.

ONCE it's cool, add the mixture to a blender along with the onion, ginger, and garlic and blend until smooth. Pour it in a medium mixing bowl and add the gochugaru, mushroom seasoning powder, sambal, vinegar, scallions, and ¼ cup water. Stir well.

USE gloved hands or a spoon to spread a thin layer of the chili mixture between each leaf of the cabbage. Use tongs to transfer the cabbage to a wide-mouthed 2-quart glass jar. Add any remaining chili mixture to the jar.

USE a spoon to push down on the mixture so the liquid rises to submerge or nearly submerge the vegetables. Cover with plastic wrap, pressing it against the surface of the mixture, then add a small weight. Cover tightly with a lid and let it ferment at room temperature (see page 2) until bubbles appear in the jar and the kimchi has soured slightly, 3 to 5 days, burping the container after 3 days.

AFTER it's fermented to your liking, store it in the fridge for up to 6 weeks.

STUFFED CABBAGE KIMCHI

MAKES ABOUT 2 QUARTS

I learn so much every time I go to Korea. On my first trip, I learned how much I didn't know about kimchi. Just when I thought I'd wrapped my head around all the varieties, I'd stroll through a market or sit down at a restaurant and find one I hadn't seen before. One of the most memorable ones came stacked in a small bowl, a miniature lasagna of cabbage leaves layered with strips of carrot, pearly pine nuts, and red dried jujubes.

It was a variety of a variety, a stuffed kimchi that was also a white kimchi, the kind that omits the bright-red, hot chili flakes that both color and ignite the versions many Americans (including, for a long time, me) associate with the pickle. Without heat, the mild tang of fermentation hits a little different, and the filling—carrots, walnuts, and dates, in my imagining—offers a bunch of textures and flavors.

One 2½- to 3-pound Napa cabbage

70 grams (½ cup) Diamond Crystal kosher salt

½ red bell pepper, cut into matchsticks (about ⅓ cup)

1 small carrot, cut into matchsticks (about ¼ cup)

¼ cup chopped (1-inch) garlic chives

6 Medjool dates, halved, pitted, and cut into ¼-inch strips

¼ cup roughly chopped toasted walnuts

1 Asian pear or 2 Bosc pears, peeled, cored, and very roughly chopped

1 cup roughly chopped white onion

4 medium garlic cloves, peeled

1 teaspoon finely chopped ginger

REMOVE any bruised leaves from the cabbage and trim any brown stuff from the bottom, but don't cut off the visible core. Quarter the cabbage through the core so the quarters stay intact, and put them in a large mixing bowl.

ADD ⅓ cup of the salt in stages, rubbing it onto the cabbage and between the cabbage leaves, until you've used it all. Set aside for 20 minutes, while the salt draws out some liquid from the cabbage. Flip the cabbage quarters and set aside for another 20 minutes.

WHILE the cabbage sits, combine the pepper, carrots, chives, dates, and walnuts in a medium mixing bowl, toss well, and set aside. In a large mixing bowl, combine 4 cups water with the remaining 3 tablespoons salt and stir to dissolve the salt. Puree the pear, onion, garlic, ginger, and 1 cup of the salty water in a blender until smooth, stir it into the rest of the salty water, and let this brine sit for 15 minutes or so.

RINSE the cabbage under cold running water and put it in a colander, giving the quarters a gentle squeeze to help drain. Tuck the date mixture between the leaves of the cabbage quarters as best you can. Add the cabbage quarters, core ends first, to a clean 2-quart glass jar, then add what's left of the date mixture. Put a fine-mesh strainer on top and pour in the brine, discarding the solids.

COVER with plastic wrap, pressing it against the surface of the mixture, then add a small weight. Cover tightly with a lid and let it ferment at room temperature (see page 2) until it sours slightly, 2 to 3 days.

AFTER it's fermented to your liking, store it in the fridge for up to 4 weeks.

QUICK RED CABBAGE KIMCHI

Ready right away or fermented for a few days, this kimchi takes its cues from the bright, fresh, briefly fermented pickle that was always in a big jar on the counter at the old Vanessa's Dumplings, on Eldridge, where I'd eat on days off during my early days living in New York.

It was on my mind when I started giving red cabbage the kimchi treatment. The result fell somewhere between baek-kimchi (aka white kimchi) and fiery red. You can eat it right away and it's almost like a dressed salad, with the koji contributing some of the umami that you'd otherwise get from fermenting. Or you can leave it for a few days and let it develop a little tang.

Note: The weights here are important. See why on page 2.

1½ pounds red cabbage, cored and cut into 1-inch pieces

20 grams (2 tablespoons plus 1 teaspoon) Diamond Crystal kosher salt

1 tablespoon plus 1 teaspoon shio koji (creamy white koji)

6½ ounces coarsely shredded white or yellow onion

5 ounces coarsely shredded Korean radish, daikon, or red radish

2 tablespoons soy sauce

2 tablespoons plus 2 teaspoons gochugaru (Korean chili flakes)

2 tablespoons finely chopped garlic

2 tablespoons finely chopped ginger

2 tablespoons toasted sesame seeds

COMBINE the cabbage, salt, and koji in a large mixing bowl. Spend a good minute or so mixing the ingredients and firmly massaging the salt into the cabbage until it starts to soften. Let it hang out for 20 minutes, stirring occasionally, to draw some of the liquid from the cabbage. Add the onion, radish, soy sauce, gochugaru, garlic, ginger, and sesame seeds and stir well. This kimchi can be enjoyed immediately or fermented.

IF you want to ferment it, transfer to a clean 2-quart glass jar, let it sit in the jar for 20 minutes or so, then use a spoon to push down on the mixture so the liquid rises to submerge or nearly submerge the vegetables. Cover with plastic wrap, pressing it against the surface of the mixture, then add a small weight. Cover tightly with a lid and let it ferment at room temperature (see page 2) until it sours slightly, 2 to 4 days, burping the container after 3 days.

AFTER it's fermented to your liking, store it in the fridge for up to 4 weeks.

KOJI CHIVE KIMCHI

MAKES ABOUT 5 CUPS

I typically over-order when I'm out for Korean, because I love the leftovers. Once, my stash included a container of garlic chives that we had tossed at the table in a thick fiery dressing and that I had accidentally left out on the counter. By the time I tried it again, it had transformed into a new thing altogether—what had been a sort of fresh salad of the pungent allium had wilted, mellowed, and soured in a really pleasant way.

Now I like to treat that accidental discovery as the goal, tumbling the chives with the dressing and adding umami-rich koji as a vegan way to help with flavor and fermentation. It's tasty without fermenting, too.

1 pound garlic chives (about 3 bunches), bottoms trimmed, cut into 1-inch pieces (8 cups)

¼ cup shio koji (creamy white koji)

1 tablespoon glutinous rice flour or all-purpose flour

1 teaspoon granulated sugar

4 ounces thin half-moon slices yellow or white onion (1 cup)

4½ ounces gochugaru (Korean chili flakes), ½ cup

¼ cup soy sauce

2 tablespoons toasted sesame seeds

COMBINE the chives and koji in a large mixing bowl and toss gently but well to evenly coat the chives with the koji. Let it hang out for 30 minutes.

MEANWHILE, combine the rice flour with 1 cup water in a small saucepan. Set it over high heat, whisking often, until it reaches a boil. Add the sugar, stir well, then pour the mixture into a heatproof bowl to cool. When it's fully cooled, add the onion, gochugaru, soy sauce, and sesame seeds and stir well. Scrape the mixture into the bowl with the chives and toss gently but well to evenly dress the chives.

TRANSFER to a clean 2-quart glass jar. Use a spoon to push down on the mixture so the liquid rises to submerge or nearly submerge the vegetables. Cover with plastic wrap, pressing it against the surface of the mixture, then add a small weight. Cover tightly with a lid and let it ferment at room temperature (see page 2) until it sours slightly, 4 to 7 days, burping the container after 3 days.

AFTER it's fermented to your liking, store it in the fridge for up to 4 weeks.

"INSTANT RAMYEON" KIMCHI

MAKES ABOUT 4 CUPS

On a night when a serious kimchi craving hit but I didn't have any in my apartment, I went rummaging through what at the time was a pretty desolate fridge and pantry for a quick fix. What I found wouldn't add up to proper kimchi but might provide some of the components—spiciness from serrano chilies rather than the more common gochugaru, tang from vinegar, and umami from a packet of seasonings from instant ramyeon rather than from lacto-fermentation. The result was so good I started making it even when my fridge was fully stocked.

My first try used standard green cabbage and lemon, but as I made it, I upgraded to Chinese/Taiwanese flat cabbage for its exceptional crunch and sweetness and looked to citric acid to give the kimchi a Flamin'-Hot-Cheetos-like pucker.

1 pound Chinese cabbage, cored and cut into 1-inch pieces (about 6 cups)

½ cup grated white or yellow onion

2 tablespoons finely chopped serrano or Thai bird chilies

14 grams (1½ tablespoons) Diamond Crystal kosher salt

1 individual vegan instant-ramyeon seasoning packet (2 tablespoons)

2 tablespoons unseasoned rice vinegar

1 teaspoon citric acid or an additional 1 tablespoon rice vinegar

COMBINE the cabbage, onion, chilies, salt, and ramyeon seasoning in a large mixing bowl. Spend a good minute or so mixing the ingredients and firmly massaging the salt into the vegetables, until they start to soften and wilt to about half their original volume. Let it hang out for 20 minutes, stirring occasionally, to draw some more of the liquid from the cabbage.

IN a small mixing bowl, stir together the vinegar and citric acid, then add to the cabbage mixture and stir well. Eat instantly.

DILLY DANDELION GREENS

MAKES ABOUT 6 CUPS

I love how this recipe pairs the bitter, very-green quality of dandelion (cut with the mild sweetness of Chinese broccoli) with a bottom-of-the-dill-pickle-jar tang. The rice flour porridge expedites the fermentation, which, with the addition of gochugaru, makes this feel at home in the kimchi category.

Note: The weights here are important. See why on page 2.

20 grams (2 tablespoons plus 1 teaspoon) Diamond Crystal kosher salt, plus more for the boiling water

1 pound Chinese broccoli or broccoli rabe, bottom ¼ inch trimmed

1 pound dandelion greens, bottom ¼ inch trimmed

4½ ounces dill (1 bunch), bottom ¼ inch trimmed

1 tablespoon glutinous rice flour or all-purpose flour

1 teaspoon granulated sugar

1 lemon

2 tablespoons gochugaru (Korean chili flakes)

1 teaspoon MSG

BRING a large pot of generously salted water to a boil over high heat and set up a big bowl of ice water. Slice the broccoli stems on the bias into long, ¼-inch-thick pieces. Keep the leaves whole.

ADD the broccoli to the boiling water, stir, and cook until the stems are tender, about 1 minute. Transfer to the ice water. Add the dandelion greens and dill, stir, and cook until bright green, 15 to 30 seconds. Transfer to the ice water and let cool completely. Drain, firmly squeeze out as much liquid as you can, then transfer to a large mixing bowl.

COMBINE the rice flour with 1 cup water in a small saucepan. Set it over high heat, whisking often, until it reaches a boil. Add the sugar, stir well, then pour the mixture into a heatproof bowl to cool. When it's fully cooled, finely grate the lemon's zest into the bowl and then squeeze in its juice. Stir in the gochugaru, 1½ tablespoons salt, and the MSG. Scrape the mixture into the bowl with the greens and toss gently but well.

TRANSFER the mixture to a clean 2-quart glass jar. Use a spoon to push down on the mixture so the liquid rises to submerge or nearly submerge the vegetables. Cover with plastic wrap, pressing it against the surface of the mixture, then add a small weight. Cover tightly with a lid and let it ferment at room temperature (see page 2) until it sours slightly, 4 to 7 days, burping the container after 3 days.

AFTER it's fermented to your liking, store it in the fridge for up to 4 weeks.

TANGERINE KIMCHI

MAKES ABOUT 1½ CUPS

By the time I went to Korea for the first time, I knew that kimchi wasn't just made from cabbage. There was kimchi made from radishes and cucumbers, pumpkin and mustard greens. You could ferment almost anything and make kimchi. On that trip, though, I realized I still had a lot to learn and that kimchi didn't need to be fermented at all. Because I frequently ate dishes that friends, hosts, and waiters called kimchi but were essentially just ingredients dressed in the pungent, often fiery red paste used to make those fermented preparations and instead eaten right away. Later, I learned this type of kimchi has a name: geotjeori.

I came home and immediately started experimenting, applying a gochugaru-fueled paste to many vegetables and fruits, including tangerines, which quickly became my favorite. The super-sweet, easy-to-separate segments go so well with the pungent, spicy dressing, and it's perfect alongside rich dishes like Sweet Sticky Rice Lotus Leaf Parcels (page 195) and Potato and Perilla Leaf Stew (page 103) and mild-mannered ones like Mino's Lentil Soup (page 109). Call this a condiment or salad or kimchi or what you'd like, as long as you make it.

Note: Don't toss those tangerine peels! Inspired by Camille Fourmont, who runs the natural wine bar and insanely good snacks shop La Buvette in Paris, I turn those peels into a vibrant powder. At the restaurant, I use a dehydrator, but at home, a low oven does the trick, as you'll see in the recipe below. A dusting elevates the tangerine kimchi, and, as Camille does with her mandarin peel powder, creamy balls of burrata drizzled with olive oil.

¼ cup gochujang (Korean red chili paste)

¼ cup Korean rice syrup, corn syrup, or maple syrup

1½ teaspoons gochugaru (Korean chili flakes)

1½ teaspoons distilled white vinegar

½ teaspoon soy sauce

½ teaspoon granulated sugar

½ teaspoon Mushroom Seasoning Powder, homemade (page 231) or store-bought

2 tablespoons thin half-moon slices white onion

1⅓ cups tangerine, clementine, or mandarin segments, peels reserved

½ cup chopped (1-inch) chives

MAKE THE TANGERINE POWDER (OPTIONAL):

PREHEAT the oven to 200°F.

CUT or use a spoon to scrape as much white pith from the reserved peels as you can (a little is OK), then tear them into approximately 2-inch pieces. Lay the peels on a single layer on a large sheet pan lined with parchment paper and dry them in the oven until the peels are completely brittle all the way through but not brown, about 45 minutes.

LET the peels cool completely, then buzz, in batches if necessary, in a blender or spice grinder to a fine powder. If you're not using it that day, transfer to the freezer, where it'll keep for up to one month. You might want to buzz it again briefly if it's in clumps.

MAKE THE TANGERINE KIMCHI:

IN a large mixing bowl, combine the gochujang, rice syrup, gochugaru, vinegar, soy sauce, sugar, and mushroom seasoning powder and stir well. Add the onion, stir well, then let sit for a couple minutes to soften its sharpness a bit. Add the tangerine segments and chives and toss gently but well.

IF you're using the tangerine powder, put about 1 tablespoon in a mesh strainer and tap it against your palm to sift the powder over the kimchi.

PICKLES

PASSION FRUIT CUCUMBER PICKLES

I don't even know if I should call this a pickle. You just toss cucumber, onion, and chilies with a little salt and sugar, let it all soften and cure for 10 minutes, then you scoop on fresh passion fruit. So it's more of a salad? Anyway, the sour, fragrant jellylike pulp stands in for the vinegar in a more classic pickle, and the crunchy seeds that the pulp clings to bring great texture. I like to eat it all right away, when the cucumber is at its crispest and the passion fruit is at its most impactful.

4 cups ¼-inch half-moon slices English cucumber (about 2)

1 cup thin half-moon slices white onion

2 tablespoons finely chopped spicy fresh chili, such as habanero, serrano, or Thai

1 tablespoon kosher salt

1 teaspoon granulated sugar

½ cup passion fruit pulp (from 3 to 4 fruits)

1 teaspoon white soy sauce or regular soy sauce

IN a large mixing bowl, toss together the cucumber, onion, chili, salt, and sugar. Let it hang out until the cucumbers release some of their liquid and soften, about 10 minutes. Drain off any liquid. Mix in the passion fruit and white soy sauce.

EAT it right away.

GREEN CHILI PICKLES

MAKES ABOUT 1 QUART

I use these brined then fermented pickles to bring heat, umami, and acidity to soups and stews, but I wouldn't hesitate to tuck them into a sandwich. They're also excellent dressed in sweet, spicy sauce and served as banchan. Jalapeños work great, but serranos are more reliably spicy, and you definitely want some fire here.

1 pound whole serrano or small jalapeño chilies

½ cup soy sauce

¼ cup distilled white vinegar

¼ cup granulated sugar

¼ cup kosher salt

USE a toothpick to poke a few deep holes in the top of each chili, just below the stem. Arrange them, stem-sides up, in a heatproof 1-quart jar.

IN a medium saucepan, bring the soy sauce, vinegar, sugar, salt, and 1½ cups water to a boil over medium-high heat, stirring to dissolve sugar and salt. Pour the hot brine over the chilies. Let cool to room temperature.

COVER with plastic wrap, pressing it against the surface of the mixture, then add a small weight (like a ramekin or very small jar). Cover tightly with a lid and let it ferment at room temperature (see page 2) for 24 hours. Then pour the liquid into a medium pot, leaving the chilies in the jar, and bring it to a rapid boil. Let the brine cool completely, then pour it back over the chilies.

ADD the weight back to the jar, then cover with a lid and leave the chilies at room temperature until they've soured to your liking, 4 to 6 days. They keep in an airtight container in the fridge for up to 4 weeks.

PETER'S PICKLED PEPPERS

MAKES ABOUT 2 CUPS

During my culinary school externship at Tribeca Grill, I really wanted my coworkers to like me. Which is probably why Peter, a back waiter who'd been there for more than a decade, felt comfortable stashing his jalapeño pickles on my station. No other cook in the kitchen would've let him.

He'd bust them out during family meal, which he insisted was never spicy enough. Because I provided storage, he shared them with me, and I started eating them with everything. I especially enjoyed them cold, straight from the fridge at my station, with the Dominican-style red beans, rice, steak, and avocado made by some of the cooks. The pickles were brutally hot, but also spicy, sweet, and salty, kind of like jalapeño teriyaki, I remember thinking at the time.

Peter borrowed the deep-fryer for the chilies, a classic restaurant trick for cooking practically anything quickly, but I roast them at home. From there, you just drown them in a simple brine of soy sauce and sugar. The brine is tasty, too. You can reuse it for your next batch, though beware, because it'll have picked up some of that chili heat.

1 pound jalapeño or serrano chilies, halved lengthwise

2 tablespoons extra-virgin olive oil

1 cup soy sauce

1 cup granulated sugar

PREHEAT the oven to 400°F.

RUB the chilies with the oil and arrange cut-sides down on a baking sheet. Roast until the skins blister and break and the chilies are tender, about 15 minutes. Let them cool, then transfer to a clean 1-quart jar with a tight-fitting lid.

IN a small pot, bring the soy sauce, sugar, and 1 cup water to a boil, stirring to dissolve the sugar. Pour the hot brine over the chilies in the jar. Let them cool, then cover and refrigerate until cold. I like them best chilled.

THEY keep in the fridge for up to 4 weeks.

TARTINE TOFU PICKLES

MAKES ABOUT 2 QUARTS

When I was in culinary school in San Francisco, I had a friend who worked at Tartine Bakery in the Mission. I'd visit him after hours, mainly to raid the leftover carrot pickles they serve with their pressed sandwiches. They're magical, these pickles. Whole tiny carrots infused in the perfect mix of tartness, spice, and savoriness to complement their natural sweetness.

Chad Robertson and Elisabeth Prueitt, Tartine's owners, know how I feel about those pickles and, a while back, they scribbled down the restaurant-scale recipe their cooks follow on the back of a napkin.

Thanks to them, I got to eat my favorite pickle at home (and straight from the fridge, the way I like it best). Once I'd finished the carrots, I started experimenting with the leftover brine, and my biggest success was tofu. Sautéed briefly, it absorbs just enough brine to become tangy and slightly creamy, almost like oil-cured feta.

1 pound firm tofu, drained

½ pound trimmed carrots, well cleaned but not peeled

2 tablespoons extra-virgin olive oil

1 cup distilled white vinegar

¼ cup thin half-moon slices white onion

2 garlic cloves, smashed and peeled

1 tablespoon red pepper flakes

2 teaspoons kosher salt

1 teaspoon black peppercorns

CUT the tofu into ½-inch slabs. Wrap the tofu cut-sides down in a clean kitchen towel, add a heavy skillet to weigh down the tofu, and let it hang out for 10 minutes or so. Cut the slabs into 1-inch pieces. Cut the carrots on the bias into ½-inch-thick slices.

IN two batches, heat half the oil in a medium nonstick skillet over medium heat until it's hot. Cook half the tofu in a single layer until golden brown on each side, 2 to 3 minutes per side. Transfer the pieces to paper towels to drain and repeat.

IN a medium-heavy saucepan, bring the vinegar, onion, garlic, red pepper flakes, salt, peppercorns, and 1 cup water to a boil. Add the carrots, reduce the heat, and simmer until they start to soften, about 2 minutes. Take the pan off the heat, add the tofu pieces to the brine, and let it all cool to room temperature.

TRANSFER to containers and refrigerate until cold, about 30 minutes. I like these pickles best chilled. They're great eaten right away, though the tofu takes on more of a cool feta quality after a few days in the fridge, so you should try that, too. The pickles keep in an airtight container in the fridge for up to 4 weeks.

BÁNH MÌ PICKLES

MAKES ABOUT 3 CUPS

I call them bánh mì pickles, just because that's when I first had these crunchy, sweet-tart matchsticks of carrot and daikon. But they're actually called *đồ chua*, and Vietnamese cooks serve them in all sorts of ways. I learned to make them from an excellent cook at Duc Loi in San Francisco whom everyone called Momma. They're super-easy to make—no stove necessary!—especially considering how good they are to eat. Sometimes I get cheffy and toss a few strips of citrus peel (lime or lemon, yuzu or bergamot) in with the brine.

The step of briefly massaging the vegetables with salt and sugar is what keeps them nice and crunchy.

2 cups thin carrot matchsticks (about 2 medium carrots)

2 cups very thin daikon matchsticks (about ½ medium daikon)

1 teaspoon kosher salt

2 cups plus 2 teaspoons granulated sugar

1 cup distilled white vinegar

PUT the carrots and daikon in a medium mixing bowl and sprinkle the salt and 2 teaspoons of the sugar over the vegetables. Massage the salt and sugar into the vegetables until they release some liquid, about 3 minutes. The carrots should brighten in color, and the daikon should become pliable. Rinse briefly under cold water, then use your hands to squeeze out any liquid. Transfer the vegetables to a narrow storage container.

STIR together the vinegar, ½ cup warm water, and remaining 2 cups sugar until the sugar dissolves. Pour the brine over the vegetables and let them pickle for 30 minutes at room temperature. Serve immediately or keep them in the fridge for up to 2 weeks.

SWEET-AND-SOUR SEAWEED PICKLES

MAKES ABOUT 4 CUPS

I still remember that initial bite of pickled seaweed at Muguboka, in San Francisco, where I was initiated into Korean food by banchan. Slippery and chewy, it was as new and exciting as the neon-green seaweed salad I'd had at my favorite sushi bar in Oklahoma, Sushi Neko. Muguboka's version of the classic banchan had this incredible push-and-pull effect, a sweetness that shoved your palate one way then a sourness that yanked it back.

2½ ounces dasima or dashi kombu, snipped into roughly 1-inch squares

½ cup dried miyeok or wakame

2 tablespoons dried tot or hijiki

½ cup carrot matchsticks (2 inches x ⅛ inch)

½ cup Korean radish, daikon, or red radish matchsticks (2 inches x ⅛ inch)

¾ cup plus 2 teaspoons granulated sugar

1 teaspoon kosher salt

1 tablespoon extra-virgin olive oil

1 teaspoon finely chopped ginger

2 cups unseasoned rice vinegar

1 tablespoon soy sauce

IN a medium mixing bowl, combine the dasima and enough cold water to cover. In a small mixing bowl, combine the miyeok and tot with enough warm water to cover. Let them all soak for 30 minutes, then drain well and set aside, keeping the dasima separate.

PUT the carrots and radishes in a small mixing bowl, sprinkle with 2 teaspoons of the sugar and the salt, and rub onto the vegetables. Let sit until they wilt and release some liquid, about 10 minutes. Gently squeeze to remove a little more liquid, discard all the liquid, and set them aside.

COMBINE the oil and ginger in a medium-heavy skillet. Set the pan over medium-high heat and cook until the ginger is sizzling and fragrant, about 2 minutes. Add the vinegar, soy sauce, drained dasima, and remaining ¾ cup sugar. Bring to a lively simmer, stirring occasionally, and cook until the liquid has reduced by about half and looks slightly syrupy, 10 to 12 minutes.

TURN off the heat, then stir in the drained miyeok and tot and the carrots and radishes. Let the pickles cool to room temperature. Refrigerate until cold, about 30 minutes. I like it best chilled.

IT keeps in an airtight container in the fridge for up to 4 weeks.

SOY SAUCE-PICKLED PERILLA LEAVES

MAKES 40, PLUS ABOUT 1 CUP OF DELICIOUS BRINE

If you spot fresh Korean perilla leaves, jagged-edged and green, buy them and buy a lot. Because then you can make this dynamic banchan, which is almost always in my fridge. It delivers the herb's vibrant flavor—like shiso but bolder and with an anise-y quality—tempered a bit by a salty, fiery brine. It's so delicious it has earned the Korean nickname "rice thief" because of how quickly steamed rice disappears when you have the pickle nearby. I think about this nickname every time I inhale a giant bowl in minutes, using chopsticks to pluck a pickled leaf by the stem from the jar, placing it on my bowl, using it to snatch the rice, then repeating the process until both the bowl and jar are empty.

Note: While it takes almost no time to make, it needs a day to reach its full potential.

1 cup soy sauce

¼ cup thinly sliced scallions

¼ cup granulated sugar

2 tablespoons finely chopped Thai bird or serrano chilies

2 teaspoons finely chopped garlic

2 teaspoons gochugaru (Korean chili flakes)

40 fresh perilla leaves

IN a small mixing bowl, combine the soy sauce, scallions, sugar, chili, garlic, and gochugaru and stir until the sugar dissolves. Find a 1-pint container about the same width as the perilla leaves (about 4 inches). They should lie flat, but it's OK if they fold a bit. Put 2 leaves in the bottom, top with 1 tablespoon of the soy sauce mixture, then add 2 leaves and another 1 tablespoon of the soy sauce mixture. Keep at it until you've used all the leaves. Pour on any remaining soy sauce mixture.

COVER with plastic wrap, pressing it against the surface of the mixture to make sure the leaves are submerged. Cover tightly with a lid and refrigerate for 1 day before serving.

STORE them in the fridge for up to 4 weeks.

DRIED MUSHROOM PICKLES

MAKES ABOUT 3 CUPS

This preparation of mushrooms is reminiscent of the Korean fish cake called eomuk, but my vegan friends love it, even those who avoid dishes that bring meat to mind. That's because the dish is mostly about the wonderful chewy, squidgy texture (common to both rehydrated dried mushrooms and denatured seafood) and the sweet, savory broth that they absorb as they simmer. The nose-tickling mustard is optional, but I've enjoyed it many times with the eomuk I've eaten, its bite cutting the sweetness of the broth.

The classic eomuk is usually woven onto a skewer and purchased as a snack from street stalls, but at home, these mushrooms are great as a part of a larger meal.

2 tablespoons extra-virgin olive oil

3 ounces dried shiitake (about 10 large), soaked and trimmed (see page 234)

2 cups mirin

2 cups Mushroom Stock, homemade (page 230) or store-bought

1 teaspoon Mushroom Seasoning Powder, homemade (page 231) or store-bought

1 tablespoon kosher salt

1 teaspoon soy sauce

2½ cups diced (1-inch) peeled Korean radish or daikon

Gyeoja (Korean hot mustard) or karashi (Japanese hot mustard), for serving (optional)

HEAT the oil in a large skillet over medium-high heat until almost smoking. Working in batches, cook the mushrooms in a single layer until browned on both sides, 45 seconds to 1 minute per side.

RETURN the mushrooms to the skillet, then add the mirin, stock, mushroom seasoning powder, salt, and soy sauce. Bring to a simmer, stirring and scraping to incorporate any browned bits that are stuck to the pan. Add the radish, let it return to a simmer, then cover and cook at a gentle simmer, skimming off any froth if necessary, until the radish is tender, 20 to 25 minutes. Turn off the heat and let it all cool.

IT keeps in the fridge in an airtight container for up to 1 week. If you're into the bite of hot mustard, stir some into the brine just before you serve.

SWEET BRAISED PEANUTS WITH OLD BAY

SERVES 4 TO 8

While I was helping Anthony Myint run Mission Street Food, he and I also started a pop-up called Mission Burger inside Duc Loi, a giant Asian supermarket a few storefronts away. We loved Duc Loi, and not just because the owners, Amanda and Howard, often let us use their kitchen for prep and gave us big, kind discounts on produce for MSF. During my shifts there, I bonded with the crew who worked the deli counter, where they typically made turkey wraps and bánh mì, and especially with a woman everyone called Momma.

One of her many responsibilities was tending the 20-gallon pot of raw shell-on peanuts full-blast-boiling in salty water spiked with Old Bay. Sometimes she got so busy with customers that the peanuts would burn. I offered to keep an eye on the pot for her, and in return she offered me my fill from the pot. I'd never had peanuts boiled before, and I was so into the texture, almost as soft as cooked beans, which reminds you that peanuts are legumes.

Ever since then I've served versions of these, though I usually make them pretty sweet. When I eat the peanuts, I can't help but think of Korean kongjang, the black soybeans simmered with soy sauce and sugar and served as banchan. The preparation here is a mash-up of these two and has a sweet-salty, pickle-y quality, so you'll find yourself eating more than you expect.

4 cups (1½ pounds) shelled raw peanuts

4 cups Mushroom Stock, homemade (page 230) or store-bought, or water

2 cups granulated sugar

¼ cup Old Bay Seasoning

½ teaspoon onion powder

2 lemons

No-Cook Hot Sauce (page 229) or Louisiana-style hot sauce

IN a medium pot, combine the peanuts, mushroom stock, sugar, Old Bay, and onion powder and bring to a boil over medium-high heat. Reduce the heat and cook, uncovered, at a moderate simmer until the liquid reduces by about half and the peanuts are pleasantly soft with a little texture to them, like a cooked chickpea, about 1 hour. Remove from the heat.

FINELY grate the lemon zest into the pot, then squeeze in the lemon's juice. Stir well and season with hot sauce. Serve the peanuts warm, room temp, or cold. They keep in the fridge for up to 1 week.

SMASHED CUCUMBERS WITH TINGLY GRANOLA

SERVES 4 TO 6

To make cucumbers taste extra flavorful, I use this classic Chinese technique of smashing them with the flat of a knife. It's easy, a little messy, and fun, plus it creates ragged-edged pieces that quickly absorb a bright garlicky, spicy dressing. On top I sprinkle a mouth-numbing "granola" made with fried shallots, peanuts, and pink peppercorns, which brings to mind a sort of Sichuan Chex Mix and adds a whole new level to the dish.

Make it with smashed-and-cured radishes, too. We do!

2 pounds Persian cucumbers (about 12) or 2 English cucumbers, ends trimmed

2 tablespoons kosher salt

1 teaspoon Mushroom Seasoning Powder, homemade (page 231) or store-bought

1 cup roughly chopped cilantro leaves and stems

2 garlic cloves, finely chopped

¼ cup Chinkiang vinegar

2 tablespoons toasted sesame seeds

2 tablespoons gochugaru (Korean chili flakes)

Scant 1 tablespoon granulated sugar

1 cup Tingly Granola (recipe follows)

IF you're using English cucumbers, halve them lengthwise. Otherwise, leave the cucumbers whole. Put the cucumbers on a work surface (cut-side down, if halved). Lay the flat of a chef's knife blade on the cucumbers, holding it in place with one hand. Using the heel of your other palm, firmly whack the flat of the knife to flatten the cucumbers slightly. Chop or tear the flattened cucumbers into about 1-inch pieces.

IN a medium mixing bowl, combine the cucumbers, salt, and mushroom seasoning powder and toss well. Let it hang out at room temperature for 15 minutes or in the fridge for up to 24 hours (the longer the better), so they can cure.

DRAIN the cucumbers, then add the cilantro, garlic, vinegar, sesame seeds, gochugaru, and sugar and stir well. Transfer to a plate and sprinkle with the granola. Serve immediately.

TINGLY GRANOLA

MAKES ABOUT 5½ CUPS

We call it granola, but it's really just sweet-salty crunchy stuff, with the lip-buzzing numbing effect from Sichuan peppercorn oil, that requires seconds of mixing, not hours of baking.

One 8-ounce jar (4 cups) Thai or Vietnamese fried shallots (also labeled "fried red onion")

1 cup unsalted roasted peanuts

3 tablespoons store-bought Sichuan peppercorn oil

2 tablespoons light or dark brown sugar

2 tablespoons dried goji berries

2 tablespoons Mushroom Seasoning Powder, homemade (page 231) or store-bought

2 tablespoons pink peppercorns

1 teaspoon kosher salt

½ teaspoon freshly ground black pepper

COMBINE everything in a large mixing bowl and toss well until the mushroom seasoning powder dissolves, 15 seconds or so.

IT keeps in an airtight container in the pantry for up to 1 month.

SARA'S SESAME STRING BEANS

SERVE 4 TO 6

This is the straight-up goma-ae that my partner, Sara, makes for us practically every week. It's a Japanese dish that her grandma made for her when she was a kid, and it relies on a simple sesame seed dressing that's salty, nutty, a little sweet, and just generally makes string beans impossible for me to stop eating. It tastes so clean, too, and what makes it especially welcome on my table is that my only other weekly string bean experience was my mom's casserole, which is basically the polar opposite of this dish. Speaking of mushy canned vegetables, make sure you cook the string beans briefly, just to take off the rawness, so they stay snappy.

1 pound string beans, trimmed and cut into 1-inch pieces (4 cups)

Kosher salt

1 tablespoon toasted sesame seeds, crushed in a mortar and pestle

2 tablespoons soy sauce

2 tablespoons well-stirred tahini (I love Soom)

1 teaspoon agave syrup or maple syrup

SET up a big bowl of ice water. In a large pot of generously salted boiling water, cook the string beans until they just lose their raw bite, 15 to 30 seconds. Use a strainer to transfer the beans to the ice water to cool. Drain them, then pat them very dry with a clean kitchen towel.

IN a medium mixing bowl, stir together the sesame seeds, soy sauce, tahini, agave, and 1 teaspoon salt until well combined. Add the beans and toss well. Season with salt. Serve now or keep in the fridge in an airtight container for up to 1 week.

ROASTED SWEET POTATO SALAD

SERVES 4 TO 6

At my family gatherings back home in Oklahoma, potato salad is serious business, something everyone had strong preferences about. For example, if my aunt heard that my grandma was bringing some to a party, my aunt would hustle to make a backup, lest my uncle had to choke down a relish-less version. Had I showed up back then with this potato salad, there would have been some very hard looks thrown my way. First of all, there's no mayo, plus there's sweet potatoes instead of russet and Korean pickled radish instead of pickle relish. It's really tasty, though.

I like using Okinawan purple sweet potatoes because they give the salad a psychedelic color, but feel free to use yellow-fleshed Japanese sweet potatoes, which have a similarly dense texture, or even orange sweet potatoes.

2 pounds Okinawan sweet potatoes (6 medium), scrubbed, halved lengthwise

2 teaspoons grapeseed or avocado oil

1 cup carrot matchsticks (3 inches x ¼ inch)

¼ cup thin half-moon slices white or yellow onion

2 teaspoons granulated sugar

1 teaspoon kosher salt

7 ounces yellow pickled radish, cut into ¼-inch half-moon slices (2 cups)

2 tablespoons whole grain mustard

1 juicy lemon, or more to taste

PREHEAT the oven to 350°F.

PUT the sweet potatoes cut-sides down on a baking sheet, rub them with the oil, and roast until lightly browned and fully tender, 30 to 40 minutes.

WHILE the sweet potatoes roast, put the carrots and onion in a large mixing bowl. Sprinkle on the sugar and salt, then toss and massage them for a couple of minutes, or until the carrots and onions become pliable. Discard any excess liquid, rinse with water, and drain very well. Put them back in the bowl, then add the pickles and mustard to the bowl. Finely grate the lemon peel into the bowl, then juice the lemon into the bowl. Mix well to combine, then set aside.

WHEN the sweet potatoes are done, take them out of the oven and let them hang out briefly, just until they're cool enough to handle. Scoop the flesh from the skins into the bowl (if you like to eat the skin, just chop them), then fold the warm sweet potatoes into the dressing. Season with salt and lemon juice. Serve immediately.

THE salad keeps in an airtight container in the fridge for up to 1 week.

SQUEEZED SPINACH WITH SCALLION-MISO DRESSING

SERVES 4

Some of my favorite dishes at Japanese restaurants are blanched vegetables tossed with a simple dressing, like Sara's Sesame String Beans (page 51). This recipe is in that same vein. Spinach gets a dunk in hot water, then is wrung out, so it tastes like itself. Since the cooking part is so simple, I like taking the extra step of rolling the spinach nice and tight with the kind of bamboo mat used to make sushi rolls, then slicing it for a cool presentation and easy snacking. Still, a heap of spinach drizzled with the magical dressing—savory from miso, sweet from melted scallions, and nutty from sesame oil—is just as delicious.

2 tablespoons Scallion-Miso Dip (page 224)

2 tablespoons toasted sesame oil

2 teaspoons agave syrup

Kosher salt

2 pounds baby spinach

IN a small mixing bowl, mix together the scallion-miso dip, sesame oil, and agave, and set aside.

BRING a large pot of water to a boil and salt it so it's salty but not as salty as pasta water. Fill a large mixing bowl with ice water.

WHEN the water's boiling, add the spinach, stir, and cook for 5 seconds or so. Drain well and transfer to the ice water. When it's cold, drain the spinach and use your hands to transfer it to a clean kitchen towel, wrap it tightly, and squeeze out as much water as possible.

IF you're not rolling it, just transfer it to a serving plate in a neat pile. If you're rolling it, put the bamboo rolling mat on the surface in front of you so the slats run across and cover with a piece of plastic wrap. Using about half the spinach and starting a few slats from the edge of the mat, make a tidy 1¼-inch-tall, 1¼-inch-wide pile of spinach that's almost as long as the slats. Fold the edge over the spinach and use your hands to form the mat-wrapped spinach into a tight cylinder. Transfer the cylinder to a cutting board and repeat with the remaining spinach. Use a sharp knife to slice them crosswise into 1-inch pieces, then transfer to a serving plate.

SPOON the sauce onto the spinach or serve it alongside for dipping.

DAD'S CARROT BANCHAN WITH RAISINS AND PINEAPPLE

SERVES 4 TO 6

When Korean restaurants give you the array of side dishes called banchan, there's usually one among them that's sweet and mayonnaise-y. Next to various types of kimchi, sauteed mountain vegetables, and mung bean jelly, a plate of macaroni or potato salad or various fruits coated in creamy dressing can be a surprising and comforting sight for newbies. Some people might wonder, "Is this Korean food?" I'm too busy eating it.

Actually, these mayo-spiked salads remind me of a salad my dad would get at Furr's Cafeteria, a chain of buffet restaurants in the Southwest, and one I grew to love, too. Bound by tangy, sweet dressing, carrots join plumped raisins and cubed pineapple— canned if you're feeling traditional, fresh if you don't like canned—for a tasty dish I treat as banchan at home. If you've got a spiralizer, now's a good time to bust it out and give the carrots a little flair.

½ cup raisins

2 tablespoons vegan mayo, like Vegenaise

1 heaping cup chopped fresh pineapple

2 tablespoons granulated sugar

1 teaspoon kosher salt

1 teaspoon ground black pepper

¼ teaspoon celery seeds

2 tablespoons distilled white vinegar

1 pound carrots, spiralized or coarsely grated

IN a small mixing bowl, soak the raisins in enough warm water to cover them until they plump, about 10 minutes. Drain the raisins and then roughly chop them.

IN a medium mixing bowl, combine the raisins with the mayo, pineapple, sugar, salt, pepper, celery seeds, and vinegar. Stir well with a fork, mashing the pineapple a bit as you go, then fold in the carrots. Cover and chill before serving.

IT keeps in an airtight container in the fridge for up to 1 week.

KIMCHI-MARINATED BROCCOLI RABE

SERVES 4 TO 6

Broccoli rabe goes really well with a gochugaru-fueled dressing, the kind of mixture that you might toss with vegetables before fermenting them to make kimchi. Plenty of lemon and a touch of sweetness push back against the lovely bitterness of rabe. It's delicious right away, but I especially like the way the flavors meld and mellow as it hangs out in the fridge.

1 pound broccoli rabe, woody bottoms trimmed, cut into 2-inch pieces

2 tablespoons extra-virgin olive oil

6 medium garlic cloves, thinly sliced

2 teaspoons kosher salt

¼ cup gochugaru (Korean chili flakes)

1 tablespoon soy sauce

1 tablespoon Korean rice syrup, maple syrup, or agave syrup

1 tablespoon toasted sesame oil

1 tablespoon toasted sesame seeds

1 juicy lemon

GIVE the broccoli rabe a brief rinse under cold water, shaking it to remove some but not all of the water. A little water clinging to the rabe lets it steam a bit as it cooks.

COMBINE the olive oil and garlic in a large skillet and set it over high heat. When the garlic turns light golden brown, add the broccoli rabe and cook, stirring occasionally, just until it's tender but still crisp, 30 to 45 seconds. Season with the salt, then cook for 15 seconds more. Transfer the broccoli rabe and garlic to a medium mixing bowl, leaving any liquid in the skillet and discarding it. Let it cool slightly, then pour off any liquid that pools in the bowl.

ADD the gochugaru, soy sauce, rice syrup, sesame oil, and sesame seeds as well as the finely grated zest and juice of the lemon to the bowl and toss to combine.

ENJOY it warm, or keep it in an airtight container in the fridge for up to 1 week.

SWEET AND STICKY LOTUS ROOT

SERVES 4 TO 6

Lotus root has this incredible texture, a sort of water chestnut–like crispness but with an intriguing chew. That and its cool wagon-wheel look make it one of my favorite vegetables to find in banchan, and to eat and cook in general. It makes a great vehicle for flavor, too, so for this super-snackable side, I briefly soak slices in vinegar to remove some of its starch and natural astringency and simmer it in a sweet-salty solution that becomes a sticky glaze. I call for rice syrup or corn syrup to give the sauce the consistency I'm after, but maple syrup and agave syrup still give you something well worth eating.

Note: If you have to, you can totally use the vac-packed lotus roots you'll find in some grocery stores. But to ensure that the lotus root retains that awesome crunch after cooking, your best bet is to use fresh lotus root. Look for firm, unblemished roots. Right before you use it (because it can discolor otherwise), trim off the ends, then use a knife or vegetable peeler to remove the tan skin.

1 pound lotus root

1 tablespoon distilled white vinegar

2 tablespoons extra-virgin olive oil

4 medium garlic cloves, halved lengthwise

¼ cup soy sauce

1 cup Korean rice syrup or corn syrup

2 teaspoons toasted sesame seeds

PEEL the lotus root, cut it into ½-inch-thick rounds, and put the lotus root in a large mixing bowl. Add the vinegar and enough cold water to cover the lotus root. Let it soak for 15 minutes to remove excess starch. Drain well.

COMBINE the oil and garlic in a medium-heavy pot or Dutch oven, set it over high heat, and let the garlic sizzle. Cook until the garlic is fragrant but not browned, 10 to 20 seconds.

ADD the lotus root to the pot (some crowding is OK) and cook, stirring once or twice, for 1 minute. Add the soy sauce, stir well, then add just enough water to cover, about 2 cups. Let it come to a simmer, then lower the heat to maintain a simmer and cook, covered, until the lotus root is slightly softened but still crunchy, about 10 minutes.

STIR in the rice syrup and simmer, partially covered this time, for 10 minutes. Uncover the pot, raise the heat to high, and cook, stirring occasionally, until the liquid thickens to a sticky, saucy glaze, 15 to 20 minutes.

EAT now or let it cool. It keeps in an airtight container in the fridge for up to 1 week. The lotus root tastes delicious hot or cold. Before serving, sprinkle on the sesame seeds.

MUNG BEAN PANCAKES

MAKES ABOUT TWENTY 3-INCH PANCAKES

The texture of *nokdu bindaetteok*, the Korean name for these mung bean pancakes, is what makes it so hard for me to resist: It's not mostly-crispy like pajeon, the Korean scallion pancake, or the latkes at Russ & Daughters, on the Lower East Side, but crisp-edged and tender inside like the latkes at Barney Greengrass, on the Upper West Side. Inside, vegetables like crunchy bean sprouts and kimchi add texture and flavor.

The typical sauce served alongside is a mixture of soy sauce and vinegar, but I have a little fun serving it with a whipped garlic sauce inspired by Lebanese toum.

1 teaspoon kosher salt, plus more for cooking the soybean sprouts

½ cup soybean sprouts

2 cups yellow mung beans (also labeled peeled or split), soaked for at least 6 hours or up to 12 hours

2 cups finely chopped spicy cabbage kimchi, homemade (page 14) or store-bought, squeezed to remove liquid, plus 1 cup kimchi liquid

½ cup roughly chopped gosari (Korean fern shoots), rinsed, or blanched julienned snow peas

1 tablespoon soy sauce

1 teaspoon freshly ground black pepper

Neutral oil for shallow-frying (about 1 cup)

1 tablespoon gochugaru (Korean chili flakes)

Whipped Garlic Sauce (page 220)

PREHEAT the oven to 200°F. Line a sheet pan with paper towels.

BRING a large pot of water to a boil and salt it so it's salty but not as salty as pasta water. Fill a large mixing bowl with ice water. Add the bean sprouts to the boiling water, cook for 15 seconds, then use a skimmer to transfer them to the ice water. When they're cool, lift the bean sprouts with your hands, give them a gentle squeeze, and move them to a kitchen towel to drain well.

DRAIN the mung beans, then transfer to the blender, add ½ cup of the kimchi liquid, and pulse to make a chunky mixture. Add the remaining kimchi liquid and pulse to what looks like a chunky pancake batter. Put the batter into a large mixing bowl, add the chopped kimchi, gosari, bean sprouts, soy sauce, 1 teaspoon salt, and the pepper, and stir well.

HEAT ¼ inch of oil in a large cast-iron or nonstick skillet over medium-high heat until hot. (Test the temperature by adding a little batter; when the oil is ready for the pancakes, the batter should sizzle loudly.)

COOK the pancakes in batches to avoid crowding: For each one, scoop out a packed ¼ cup of the mixture per pancake, add it to the oil, and gently flatten it to an even ½ inch or so. Cook, flipping once, until they're golden brown, crispy, and set inside, 2 to 3 minutes per side. Transfer them to the lined sheet pan as they're done and keep warm in the oven.

COOK the remaining pancakes the same way, adding more oil if necessary to maintain the depth and letting it get hot before adding the next batch.

SERVE with the garlic sauce and top with the gochugaru.

SWEET-AND-SOUR EGGPLANT

SERVES 4 TO 6

Like jjajangmyeon (page 138), tangsuyuk is another classic in the beloved Korean-Chinese food genre. Basically, it's sweet-and-sour pork adjusted for Korean tastes. And now here it is adjusted for mine. In this book, of course, there's no pork, so I focus on the sauce. The versions I've had often include cucumber and pineapple, and mine adds hibiscus to the equation for its astringent tartness and for the grape-juice-purple color it creates, which mirrors that of the eggplant.

FOR THE SAUCE

1 cup canned pineapple juice

2 tablespoons dried hibiscus flowers

¼ cup granulated sugar

¼ cup unseasoned rice vinegar

1 tablespoon potato starch

1 tablespoon soy sauce

¼ teaspoon kosher salt

½ cup all-purpose flour

½ cup potato starch

¼ teaspoon garlic powder

¼ teaspoon onion powder

1 tablespoon neutral oil, plus about 8 cups for deep-frying

¼ cup Shaoxing wine, dry white wine, or dry sake

1 teaspoon Umami Salt and Pepper (page 231)

1 teaspoon grated ginger

2 pounds Chinese eggplants (about 6), tops removed

1 cup diced (1-inch) canned pineapple

5 ounces Persian or Japanese cucumbers, cut into matchsticks (about 1 cup)

1 tablespoon toasted black or white sesame seeds

MAKE THE SAUCE:

COMBINE the pineapple juice and ½ cup water in a small pot, bring to a boil, and stir in the hibiscus flowers. Cover and steep off the heat for 15 minutes. Scoop out the hibiscus flowers, finely chop them, then add them back to the pot along with the sugar, vinegar, potato starch, soy sauce, and salt. Bring to a simmer over medium-high heat, then start whisking until it's glossy and slightly thickened, about 30 seconds. Turn off the heat and cover to keep warm.

MAKE THE DISH:

PREHEAT the oven to 200°F.

IN a medium mixing bowl, combine the flour, potato starch, garlic powder, onion powder, 1 tablespoon of the oil, and 1 cup water and stir to make a smooth, thick batter. Set aside.

IN a large mixing bowl, stir together the Shaoxing wine, umami salt and pepper, and ginger. Quarter the eggplants lengthwise, cut them crosswise into 2-inch pieces, and add to the larger bowl. Toss to coat well and set aside.

LINE a large tray with paper towels. Pour 3 inches of the oil into a large heavy-bottomed pot and bring it to 350°F (use a deep-fry thermometer) over high heat, stirring occasionally to distribute the heat.

BATTER and fry the eggplant in several batches. Add the first batch of eggplant to the bowl with the batter, toss to coat well, and, one at a time, shake gently to let the excess batter drip off and carefully add to the oil. Fry, stirring occasionally, until crunchy and golden brown, 7 to 8 minutes per batch. Transfer to the tray to drain and keep warm in the oven. Let the oil return to 350°F and fry the remaining eggplant.

PUT the fried eggplant on a plate, drizzle with the sauce, then add the pineapple, cucumber, and sesame seeds. Serve right away.

HONEY BUTTER CORN RIBS

SERVES 4 TO 6

This isn't *that* different from the sugary summer corn dunked in melted butter and sprinkled with salt I ate as a kid at the county fair in Oklahoma. Here, though, the corn comes in little riblets that curl in the oven, the cob acting like bone, a cool trick that I very much did not come up with myself. The salty-sweet sauce is based on the craze that hit South Korea some years back, when the company Haitai released a very tasty honey-butter variety of potato chips that caused more hype in Seoul than a Supreme drop in SoHo.

    Only the XXX Spice would make ten-year-old me do a double take. But I can't imagine the dish without it. The mouth-numbing effect keeps the sweetness in check, while its warm spices like clove and cardamom take that sweetness in an unexpected direction.

FOR THE XXX SPICE

2 tablespoons whole cloves

2 tablespoons fennel seeds

2 tablespoons green Sichuan peppercorns

2 tablespoons green cardamom pods

2 tablespoons Mushroom Seasoning Powder, homemade (page 231) or store-bought

2 tablespoons granulated sugar

2 tablespoons cayenne pepper

FOR THE DISH

6 ears of corn, husked

¼ cup plus 2 tablespoons extra-virgin olive oil

½ teaspoon kosher salt

½ teaspoon freshly ground black pepper

¼ cup unsalted vegan butter

2 tablespoons thinly sliced garlic

2 tablespoons soy sauce

1 teaspoon agave syrup or maple syrup

1 tablespoon aonori

MAKE THE XXX SPICE:

IN batches if necessary, grind the ingredients to a fine powder in a spice or coffee grinder. Transfer each batch to a container, and when it's all ground, stir really well.

IT keeps in your pantry for 2 months before it starts to lose its vibrancy.

MAKE THE DISH:

PREHEAT the oven to 350°F.

USE a heavy, sharp knife to cut each ear of corn into half crosswise, then quarter each half lengthwise through the cob. Trim off all but the ½ inch of the cob.

IN a large mixing bowl, combine the corn and ¼ cup olive oil and toss to coat well. Sprinkle on ¼ cup of the XXX spice, the salt, and the pepper and toss to coat evenly. Spread the corn on two large sheet pans in a single layer and bake, changing the pans' positions once halfway through, until the corn curls and browns, 15 to 20 minutes.

WHILE the corn cooks, combine the vegan butter, the remaining 2 tablespoons olive oil, and garlic in a wok or heavy skillet, set it over medium-high heat, and let the butter melt and the fat sizzle. Cook until the garlic is golden brown, about 1 minute. Turn off the heat and stir in the soy sauce and agave. Cover to keep warm.

WHEN the corn ribs are ready, drizzle on the sauce and serve right away, garnished with the aonori.

MUSHROOM BULGOGI

SERVES 4

I'm pretty sure I was the first person to make kung pao home fries (for whatever that's worth), but I'm positive I'm not blazing any trails by giving mushrooms the bulgogi treatment. It's great for both vegans and meat-eaters, since mushrooms provide umami, a satisfying chew, and a great vehicle for the sweet-salty soak made with soy sauce, aromatics, and Korean soda (or Sprite!).

   I think a combo of fresh and rehydrated dried mushrooms gives you a really nice texture, and throwing slippery glass noodles and rice cakes in the mix gives the sauce something else to hold on to. I eat the dish with rice and kimchi, but you could give it the lettuce-wrap treatment, too.

1 ounce dried shiitake (about 4 large), soaked and trimmed (see page 234)

3 ounces dried sweet potato starch noodles (dangmyeon), soaked in cold water for 30 minutes and drained well

3 tablespoons extra-virgin olive oil

2 cups sliced (½ inch) stemmed fresh shiitake (about 16)

2 tablespoons thinly sliced garlic

3 ounces (½ cup) Korean rice cake sticks, soaked in cold water for 30 minutes and drained well

¼ cup Chilsung Cider, Sprite, or ginger ale

1 tablespoon soy sauce

1½ teaspoons Mushroom Seasoning Powder, homemade (page 231) or store-bought

1 teaspoon toasted sesame oil

½ cup sliced (¼ inch) yellow or white onion

1 tablespoon grapeseed or another neutral oil

½ medium Asian pear or 1 Bosc pear, peeled, cored, and thinly sliced

1 teaspoon toasted sesame seeds

BRING a large pot of water to a boil. Meanwhile, slice the soaked mushroom caps ¼ inch thick.

ADD the sweet potato starch noodles and boil, stirring occasionally, until they're tender but still chewy, about 8 minutes. Drain, rinse under water, and drain really well. Use scissors to snip them into 1-inch pieces.

HEAT a wide cast-iron skillet over medium-high heat for a couple of minutes. Add the olive oil, then add the fresh mushrooms in a single layer and cook without stirring until the bottoms start to turn golden, 1 to 2 minutes. Add the garlic and cook, stirring, until the garlic is fragrant and light golden, 30 seconds or so.

ADD the dried mushrooms, rice cakes, Chilsung cider, soy sauce, mushroom seasoning powder, and sesame oil and cook, stirring occasionally, until the rice cakes are fully tender but still chewy and the liquid is mostly gone, about 2 minutes. Turn off the heat, stir in the sweet potato starch noodles, and transfer to a bowl for the moment.

CLEAN the cast-iron skillet, then set it over medium heat for 3 to 5 minutes, so it gets really hot. Add the onion to the skillet in a single layer, evenly drizzle on the grapeseed oil, and turn off the heat. Immediately add the mushroom-noodle mixture evenly on top of the onions. Top with the pear and sesame seeds and serve in the hot pan.

STEAMY MUSHROOMS

SERVES 4

Part of the joy of mushrooms is their incredible fragrance. Like when you order donabe at a Japanese restaurant and the waiter removes the lid and the aroma just hits you. That's on my mind whenever I make these, a mixture of mushrooms tucked into foil packets along with a compound (vegan) butter plus soy sauce and a splash of sake. After a short trip in the oven, you bring them to the table and let friends peek inside, revealing soft, steamy mushrooms and releasing that intoxicating smell.

½ cup unsalted vegan butter, softened at room temperature

½ cup finely chopped shallots

1 small garlic clove, finely chopped

1½ pounds mixed mushrooms, trimmed and torn or cut into bite-sized pieces

1½ teaspoons Umami Salt and Pepper (page 231)

¼ cup soy sauce

1 tablespoon dry sake

PREHEAT the oven to 350°F.

IN a small mixing bowl, combine the vegan butter, shallots, and garlic and stir well. Set aside.

ARRANGE the mushrooms on the center of each of four 9 x 13-inch sheets of foil in a low, tidy pile. Onto each one, sprinkle the umami salt and pepper, drizzle the soy sauce and sake, then dollop the vegan butter mixture. Fold one of the short sides over the mushrooms to meet the other side, leaving a little space above the mushrooms. Then fold the edges to seal them tightly.

SET the packets on a large sheet pan (or even better, a rack set on a sheet pan) and bake for 25 minutes. Serve hot and steamy.

SMOKY FRIED NAPA CABBAGE

SERVES 4 TO 6

As an adult I eat so much cabbage and in so many forms, but back in Oklahoma, I mostly had it only in so-called fried cabbage, a Southern standard that was basically just green cabbage sauteed with bacon. Now that I make it myself, I look to Napa cabbage, which takes on a delicate, buttery texture even though it cooks only briefly, and smoked tofu for chewy contrast. A little white wine brightens things up and chilies team up with umami salt and pepper for two kinds of heat.

¼ cup extra-virgin olive oil

3 garlic cloves, smashed and peeled

½ medium white or yellow onion, cut into 1-inch pieces

12 cups cored, chopped (1-inch pieces) Napa cabbage (about 1½ pounds)

¾ teaspoon Umami Salt and Pepper (page 231)

½ pound smoked firm tofu, finely chopped

½ cup dry white wine

3 oil-cured Calabrian chilies, stemmed and halved lengthwise

COMBINE the oil and garlic in a large Dutch oven, set over high heat, and get the garlic sizzling. Stir frequently until the garlic is toasty and golden around the edges, 1 to 2 minutes, then add the onion and cook, stirring occasionally, until translucent and a little golden, about 2 minutes.

ADD half the cabbage and cook, stirring, until slightly wilted, about 1 minute. Stir in half the umami salt and pepper, then add the rest of the cabbage, stir until it's all wilted, and stir in the remaining umami salt and pepper.

ADD the tofu, wine, and chilies and stir well. Cover the pot, reduce the heat to cook at a moderate simmer, and cook, stirring once or twice, for 5 minutes. Remove the lid and cook until the cabbage is tender and the liquid has reduced by half or so, so it's slightly saucy, about 5 minutes more. Serve right away.

WHOLE EGGPLANT "MIZNON"

SERVES 4 TO 6

A big thank-you goes to the chef Eyal Shani, who runs the group of Israeli restaurants called Miznon, for sharing this method for cooking and cutting eggplant with the world. And it's so simple to execute. You just put the eggplant in a skillet and stick it in a hot oven. The skin chars, and the flesh steams and takes on some of that burnt-skin smokiness. Then you peel off the skin and serve the creamy eggplant on a plate barely chopped.

From there, it's about saucing it up. Sometimes, I just go with tahini and a sauce of grated ripe tomato mixed with salt and olive oil to taste. But lately I've been eating it this way: topped with an acidic, garlicky condiment made with capers, mustard, and red wine vinegar that, after it mingles with the finishing drizzle of chili oil and sprinkle of chili flakes, I swear ends up tasting like the dip I make for myself at Sichuan hot pot places with the DIY sauce bars.

4 large globe eggplants

1 cup Tart Garlic Sauce (page 221), or more to taste

4 teaspoons gochugaru (Korean chili flakes), or more to taste

¼ cup Chili Oil, homemade (page 228) or store-bought

POSITION a rack near the bottom of the oven and preheat the oven to 450°F.

PUT the eggplants, whole, on a large sheet pan with plenty of space between them and bake on the bottom rack for 30 minutes, or until the skin on the bottom starts to char a bit. Carefully flip the eggplants, taking care not to break the skin, then add the pan back to the oven, rotated now to encourage even cooking. Bake until they're very soft, about 30 minutes more.

LET the eggplants cool slightly, about 10 minutes. Carefully put them on a cutting board or plate and use your fingers to peel back and remove the skin. With a large sturdy spoon supporting the bottoms so they don't fall apart, move the eggplants to a plate or platter. Gently chop the eggplants with a knife, slicing crosswise every ¼ inch or so and stopping about 2 inches from the stem, then doing the same in the other direction to make a cross-hatched pattern. It'll barely take any pressure because the eggplant will be so soft.

SPOON on the garlic sauce, then sprinkle on the chili flakes and drizzle on the chili oil.

HOT SAUCE GREENS

SERVES 4 TO 6

I've been hooked on long-cooked greens seasoned with hot sauce since I first tried them at Eddie's Café, in San Francisco. It's on Divisadero, right down the block from my old apartment, and when I lived there I went for a breakfast of collards and grits often enough that the owner, Helen Hwang, would always bring me my favorite hot sauce, Crystal, without my asking.

When I'm doing the cooking, I make this version. Instead of stewing, I go for a relatively quick saute of bright, silky chard, herbaceous chrysanthemum greens, and parsley, which delivers this really cool savory quality, especially when paired with sesame oil.

The pepperoncini, by the way, might seem out of place, yet when I cooked with Sichuan culinary legend Yu Bo, he often used a certain mild pickled chili that was particular to Chengdu but that reminded me of the pepperoncini I first encountered in diner chef's salads.

½ cup plus 2 tablespoons extra-virgin olive oil

¼ cup finely chopped garlic (about 10 cloves)

¼ cup drained sliced pepperoncini

2 bunches parsley (about 7 ounces), trimmed, stems thinly sliced, leaves whole

One 8-ounce bunch chrysanthemum greens, woody bottoms trimmed, roughly chopped

2 bunches rainbow chard (about 1½ pounds), bottoms trimmed, leaves torn in half, stems thinly sliced

2½ teaspoons kosher salt, or more to taste

1 tablespoon coarsely cracked black peppercorns

2 teaspoons toasted sesame oil

No-Cook Hot Sauce (page 229) or Crystal hot sauce

COMBINE ½ cup of the olive oil, the garlic, and pepperoncini in a wok or heavy skillet, set it over medium-high heat, and let the oil sizzle. Cook until the garlic takes on a little color, about 1 minute. Stir in the parsley and chrysanthemum greens and cook until they wilt slightly, about 30 seconds. Stir in chard leaves, toss until wilted, then stir in the chard stems, salt, and peppercorns. Reduce the heat to medium-low and cook, uncovered, until the stems are tender but still have a slight crunch to them, about 5 minutes. Season with salt.

MEANWHILE, mix together the remaining 2 tablespoons olive oil and the sesame oil in a small mixing bowl. When the greens are ready, transfer them to a serving bowl and drizzle on the sesame oil mixture. Serve with the hot sauce and plenty of rice.

WATERCRESS SALAD WITH ACORN JELLY

SERVES 6 TO 8

This salad is best served cold. And not just cold—really cold. When I had it in Seoul, on the hottest day of summer, the salad came in a chilled bowl and there were ice cubes among the crisp greens, lots of herbs, and crunchy vegetables. It was exceptionally refreshing. The acorn jelly (made from acorn starch) is tasty, too, gelatinous and bland and perfect for taking on the bright, boldly spicy dressing.

FOR THE ACORN JELLY

Vegetable oil for the pan

½ cup acorn jelly flour

½ teaspoon kosher salt

FOR THE DRESSING

⅓ cup soy sauce

¼ cup thinly sliced green onion

2 serrano chilies, sliced ¼ inch thick

2 tablespoons unseasoned rice vinegar

1 tablespoon finely chopped garlic

1 tablespoon gochugaru (Korean chili flakes)

1 tablespoon toasted sesame oil

1 tablespoon toasted sesame seeds

2 teaspoons agave syrup

FOR THE SALAD

2 cups chopped (½-inch pieces) romaine lettuce

1 cup chopped (2-inch pieces) watercress, thick stems trimmed

1 cup chopped (1-inch pieces) chrysanthemum greens

1 cup torn perilla leaves or a combo of dill fronds and mint leaves

¼ cup thin half-moon slices white or yellow onion

¼ cup julienned (¼ inch x 3 inches) cucumber

¼ cup julienned (¼ inch x 3 inches) carrot

Crushed ice, for serving (optional)

MAKE THE JELLY:

LIGHTLY oil a 3½- to 4-cup heatproof glass container or Bundt pan.

COMBINE the flour and salt in a medium saucepan, then whisk in 3 cups water until smooth and lump-free. Bring to a simmer over medium-high heat, whisking, until large bubbles form on the surface like polenta and the mixture thickens to the consistency of pancake batter, about 5 minutes.

TRANSFER to the oiled container and let it cool completely until it sets. Cover and refrigerate until chilled, at least 1 hour or up to 5 days.

MAKE THE DRESSING:

STIR together all the dressing ingredients in a medium mixing bowl.

MAKE THE SALAD:

INVERT the container of jelly onto a cutting board, then cut the jelly into bite-sized pieces. Put them in a large mixing bowl with all the salad ingredients. Pour on the dressing and toss well.

SERVE immediately on chilled plates and top with a little crushed ice.

TIGER SALAD

SERVES 4 TO 6

Like a lot of New Yorkers, I know about tiger salad thanks to Xi'an Famous Foods. What started as a stall in Flushing's Golden Shopping Mall run by Jason Wang and his father became an operation with eight locations in three boroughs, all serving the same excellent food inspired by those of the restaurant's namesake city in China's Shaanxi province. Before they took it off the menu, I pretty much always ordered their tiger salad—a lightly dressed pile of cilantro, scallions, celery, and green chilies that explodes with fresh, green flavor and works as a good foil for rich, oily stuff. At Mission, we used to make a complicated version with mussels and rice noodles, but nowadays I'm really into this version, a slightly different collection of greenery from Xi'an's, with a dressing that uses blended red radishes for body and sweetness in addition to citrus and ultra-fragrant yuzu kosho.

Note: A spicy, salty fermented paste made from the zest of fragrant Japanese citrus called yuzu and chilies (in this case red ones), yuzu kosho makes a phenomenal addition to your pantry. Look for products made without preservatives, like the Ocean Foods brand. The ingredients should be just yuzu zest, chili, and salt.

FOR THE DRESSING

¼ pound trimmed red radishes (about 4), very roughly chopped

1½ tablespoons white soy sauce

¼ cup unseasoned rice vinegar

1½ teaspoons lemon juice

1½ teaspoons lime juice

½ teaspoon red yuzu kosho

FOR THE SALAD

1 cup thinly sliced scallions

4 cups loosely packed watercress, arugula, or other peppery greens

1 cup loosely packed basil leaves (Thai or Italian)

1 cup loosely packed roughly chopped cilantro

1 cup loosely packed mint leaves

1 teaspoon toasted sesame seeds

MAKE THE DRESSING:

PUT the dressing ingredients in a blender with ¼ cup water and blend on high speed until very smooth.

IT keeps in an airtight container in the fridge for up to 1 week, though it'll get increasingly pungent.

MAKE THE SALAD:

FILL a medium mixing bowl with ice water, add the scallions, and let them soak for 5 minutes, to get them crisp. Drain well and gently squeeze out the excess water.

COMBINE the scallions, watercress, basil, cilantro, mint, sesame seeds, and ¾ cup of the dressing (or more to taste), toss, and serve.

STEWS AND SOUPS

MAPO TOFU

SERVES 4 TO 6

Mapo tofu has been on the menu since back when Mission Chinese Food first popped up in San Francisco. Over the years, we've tweaked the recipe approximately one hundred times, and this vegan version is the best yet, not to mention the easiest for the home cook. What used to take days to make is ready in less than an hour.

Note: This recipe calls for doubanjiang, a coarse reddish paste of fermented soybeans, broad beans, and chilies common in Sichuan cooking. Look for "Pixian" on the label, which means it hails from a town in Sichuan province known for making the product.

2 cups (2½ ounces) dried shiitake

2 tablespoons Mushroom Seasoning Powder, homemade (page 231) or store-bought

Scant 1 tablespoon granulated sugar

Kosher salt

3 pounds soft silken tofu, drained and cut into 1½-inch cubes

2 tablespoons cornstarch

1 cup olive, canola, or grapeseed oil

½ cup tomato paste

½ cup Sichuan doubanjiang (chili-bean paste)

½ cup finely chopped garlic (about 3 ounces)

½ cup finely chopped ginger (about 2¼ ounces)

2 tablespoons Black Bean Sauce (page 226)

3 tablespoons gochugaru (Korean chili flakes)

3 tablespoons store-bought Sichuan peppercorn oil

3 tablespoons Sichuan peppercorn powder, or more to taste

½ cup Chili Oil, homemade (page 228) or store-bought

2 cups loosely packed roughly chopped cilantro

1 cup loosely packed roughly chopped Chinese yellow chives

PUT the mushrooms in a heatproof bowl along with the mushroom seasoning powder, sugar, and 1 tablespoon salt. Pour in 2 cups boiling water, stir, and soak for 20 minutes.

MEANWHILE, bring a medium pot of salted water (a few generous pinches should do it) to a boil. Add the tofu, let the water return to a boil, then drain the tofu gently and well. (This helps flavor the tofu and keeps it from falling apart later.) In a small mixing bowl, stir together the cornstarch and ¼ cup water and set it aside.

DRAIN the mushrooms, reserving the liquid in a bowl. Use scissors to snip off and discard the tough stem nubs, gently squeeze the mushrooms over the bowl to remove excess liquid, then chop the mushrooms into ¼- to ⅛-inch pieces.

IN a large heavy pot, heat the oil over high heat until it smokes. Add the chopped mushrooms and cook, stirring, until they brown a bit, about 2 minutes. Stir in the tomato paste and cook, stirring, until it begins to stick to the pot, 2 to 3 minutes more. Stir in the doubanjiang, garlic, ginger, and black bean sauce and cook for a minute or two, then stir in the gochugaru and the reserved mushroom soaking liquid. Let come to a boil over high heat, then reduce the heat to gently simmer and stir in the Sichuan peppercorn oil and Sichuan peppercorn powder.

WHILE stirring, drizzle in the cornstarch mixture, increase the heat, and let come to a boil. Reduce the heat slightly and add the tofu. Cook, stirring gently so the cubes are coated in the sauce but stay more or less intact, until warmed through, 1 to 2 minutes. Serve it with rice and garnish bowls with the chili oil, herbs, and another sprinkle of Sichuan peppercorn powder to taste.

MAPO RAMEN

SERVES 4

I didn't come up with this one, even though it seems like something a chef who almost always has ramen and mapo tofu on the menu might've invented. As far as I can tell, it was cooks in Tokyo with a thing for both who thought to combine the two, thus kicking off the trend in Japan and beyond.

I prefer instant noodles (either ramen or Korean ramyeon) when I make mapo ramen, and I use the seasoning packets to increase the explosive force of the umami bomb. Tahini and vegan butter add richness that helps to carry all that flavor while also toning down the big, salty, mouth-numbing intensity just enough so you can take down an entire bowl yourself.

Because I'm a fan of a little carb-on-carb action, I eat mine with rice on the side.

3 tablespoons well-stirred tahini (I love Soom)

1½ tablespoons unseasoned rice vinegar

1 teaspoon soy sauce

Four 4-ounce packages vegan instant ramen or ramyeon, including the seasoning packets

2 tablespoons unsalted vegan butter

4 cups Mapo Tofu (page 90), hot

1 cup chopped chive

IN a small mixing bowl, stir together the tahini, vinegar, and soy sauce until smooth and set aside.

BRING a large pot of water to a boil. Add the noodles to the boiling water, stir well, and cook until tender but with a slight bite, a bit less than the package instructions say.

DRAIN the noodles, reserving 1 cup of the cooking water. In the pot, combine the cooking water, tahini mixture, and the contents of all four seasoning packets and stir well. Add the noodles and vegan butter and cook over low heat, tossing, until the butter has melted.

SERVE in bowls topped with the mapo tofu and chives.

QUICK DOENJANG STEW

SERVES 4

In my apartment, this stew is always on the stove or in the fridge. I eat it almost every morning, often with rice and kimchi. It's simple and flavorful, the broth invigorated by both fresh and dried chili heat as well as the bold flavor of doenjang (Korean fermented soybean paste) or Japanese miso, which I happily use if that's what I have on hand. It's hearty, too, packed with wonderfully bland tofu and summer squash, which gets soft and juicy as it sucks up the soup's flavor and contributes some of its own in return.

It's a great canvas for what you have in the fridge. You can use whatever vegetables you want. Winter squash in place of the summer squash, garlic for the ginger, leeks for the onions. Sometimes, I'll throw in greens like spinach, kale, or lettuce right at the end, letting them wilt.

5 cups Mushroom Stock, homemade (page 230) or store-bought

¼ cup doenjang or miso (white, red, whatever you've got)

1 pound firm tofu, drained and cut into 1-inch cubes

½ pound trimmed green and/or yellow summer squash, cut into 1-inch cubes

1 small russet potato, peeled, quartered, and sliced ¼ inch thick (1 cup)

1 cup diced (1 inch) white onion

¼ cup finely chopped ginger (a fat 4-inch knob)

2 tablespoons finely chopped serrano chilies

1 tablespoon gochugaru (Korean chili flakes)

Kosher salt

IN a small mixing bowl, combine 2 tablespoons of the mushroom stock with the doenjang and stir until smooth.

TO a medium pot, add the remaining stock as well as the tofu, squash, potato, onion, ginger, chilies, and gochugaru. Stir in the doenjang mixture, and bring to a boil over high heat. Reduce the heat to cook at a gentle simmer until the vegetables are soft, about 10 minutes. Season with salt. Serve hot.

KIMCHI STEW

SERVES 4 TO 6

When I was first getting into Korean food, I was all about barbecue. Then one time when I was ordering, I threw in kimchi-jjigae as a sort of why-not dish and my eyes opened to the huge range of glorious soups and stews. It made quite an impact on me. The complex tang and funk that's the stew's driving force comes from kimchi that's been fermented for a while. If you buy kimchi at a Korean market, ask someone to point you to kimchi that's good for soups and stews. If you already have kimchi in your fridge, keep in mind that it will continue to gradually ferment and it's perfect for stews and soups when it tastes notably sour, loses its crunch, and occasionally gets slightly effervescent.

The good news when you get to cooking is that the kimchi maker already did most of the work for you, so it's ready in no time. For texture and because it's my favorite flavor sponge, I look to chewy Japanese inari, tofu that's been double-fried and marinated, in place of the classic pork belly.

3 scallions, trimmed

4 cups chopped spicy cabbage kimchi, homemade (page 14) or store-bought, plus 1 cup kimchi juice

1 yellow or white onion, thinly sliced

1 pound firm tofu, drained and cut into 1-inch cubes

3 serrano chilies, cut into ¼-inch-thick slices

2 cups drained inari

¼ cup extra-virgin olive oil

1 tablespoon Mushroom Seasoning Powder, homemade (page 231) or store-bought

1 tablespoon finely chopped garlic

1 tablespoon finely chopped ginger

1 tablespoon gochugaru (Korean chili flakes)

1 tablespoon toasted sesame oil

1 teaspoon kosher salt, or more to taste

PUT the scallions on a work surface and use the flat of a chef's knife blade to firmly whack the whites to smash them. Cut the scallions into 1-inch pieces.

IN a medium Dutch oven, add the kimchi and its liquid as a layer first, then add the onion in a layer, then the tofu, then the scallions and chilies, and finally the inari.

IN a medium mixing bowl, combine the olive oil, mushroom seasoning powder, garlic, ginger, gochugaru, sesame oil, salt, and 4 cups water and stir well. Pour the mixture evenly over the layers in the pot.

PUT the pot over high heat and bring it to a boil. Cover, reduce the heat, and cook at a moderate simmer, without stirring, until the onions are tender, about 10 minutes. Season with salt. Serve hot.

SPICY SILKEN TOFU STEW

SERVES 4 TO 6

Making sundubu-jjigae in my tiny kitchen in Manhattan's Chinatown makes me think of how different my life is now from when I was a kid in Oklahoma. I grew up on stews that were essentially just beef, carrots, and potatoes flavored with tomato paste and bouillon. Now, I get to eat in Technicolor, slurping up broths fragrant with ginger and garlic and electrified by chilies. This dish is as loud and light as the stews from my mom's Crock-Pot were tame and heavy.

The flavor-packed broth is a thrill, but the mushrooms and tofu are also a draw. While soft tofu is OK in a pinch, the move here is to find sundubu sold in tubes (and sometimes cartons labeled "extra silken"), which is so wobbly it makes the merely soft stuff seem like rubber. You just snip off one end and let the tofu slide into the broth. Since there's no meat or egg in mine, I spoon on sesame oil mixed with Korean chili flakes and umami-stuff right at the end to add some fat and to keep the heat nice and bright.

Eat it with heaps of rice and piles of kimchi.

FOR THE FINISHING OIL

¼ cup toasted sesame oil

2 tablespoons gochugaru (Korean chili flakes)

1 tablespoon toasted sesame seeds

1 tablespoon Umami Salt and Pepper (page 231)

FOR THE STEW

5 scallions, trimmed

¼ cup extra-virgin olive oil

1 tablespoon finely chopped garlic

1 tablespoon finely chopped ginger

3 cups chopped (about ½ inch) mixed fresh mushrooms

1 cup thinly sliced white onion

4 cups Mushroom Stock, homemade (page 230) or store-bought

¼ cup minced jarred pepperoncini, plus ½ cup brine from the jar

2 tablespoons minced fresh Thai bird chilies (about 8) or serrano chilies (about 4)

½ teaspoon kosher salt

½ teaspoon soy sauce

12 ounces sundubu or soft silken tofu, drained if necessary

Charred Red Chili Paste (page 222), optional, for serving

STIR everything together and set aside.

MAKE THE STEW:

PUT the scallions on a work surface and use the flat of a chef's knife blade to firmly whack the whites to smash them. Thinly slice the scallions.

IN a dolsot (stone pot) or other medium-heavy pot, combine the olive oil, garlic, and ginger, set over medium-high heat, and let it sizzle. Cook, stirring, until fragrant but not colored, 30 seconds to 1 minute. Add the scallions, mushrooms, onion, stock, pepperoncini, chilies, salt, and soy sauce, then raise the heat and bring to a boil, skimming the froth.

SQUEEZE in the sundubu (or spoon in the silken tofu in four big pieces), then reduce the heat and cook at a gentle simmer, without stirring, until the onions are tender and the tofu is hot, about 5 minutes. Stir in the finishing oil and serve with the chili paste.

NOT-SPICY SILKEN TOFU STEW

SERVES 4

Until I went to Korea, all the sundubu-jjigae (soft-tofu stew) I'd eaten had come with a red tint from gochugaru, and with it the promise that I'd be dabbing my forehead after a few slurps. But in Korea I also developed an affection for the milder versions. They are still full of flavor with super-savory broth and the same custardy, wobbly soft tofu.

When I try to re-create the bowls I've enjoyed most, I dig into my pantry and my memories. I look to wine for a little brightness, fresh green chilies for a bit of grassy heat, and tahini to add sesame flavor to the stew but also body to the broth, which the versions I've tried achieved using everything from egg to ground perilla seeds. And since I'm so into how Korean cooks add ssukgat (chrysanthemum greens) to brothy dishes, I do it here, tossing them in a bright-green puree of parsley, an herb that might not be common in Korean cooking but which I'm pretty sure I've been served, blanched and dressed, as banchan.

FOR THE PARSLEY DRESSING

1 cup roughly chopped parsley

¼ cup extra-virgin olive oil

2 tablespoons toasted sesame oil

1½ teaspoons Umami Salt and Pepper (page 231)

FOR THE STEW

3 tablespoons well-stirred tahini (I love Soom)

2 tablespoons unseasoned rice vinegar

1 teaspoon soy sauce

¼ cup extra-virgin olive oil

3 long green chilies, quartered lengthwise and chopped into ½-inch pieces

2 garlic cloves, sliced ¼ inch thick

A fat 2-inch knob ginger, peeled and sliced ¼ inch thick

¼ cup dry white wine

4 cups Mushroom Stock, homemade (page 230) or store-bought or store-bought

24 ounces sundubu or soft silken tofu, drained if necessary

¾ pound chrysanthemum greens or watercress, woody bottoms trimmed, roughly chopped

MAKE THE PARSLEY DRESSING:

COMBINE the ingredients in a blender, pulse until the parsley is more or less submerged in the oil, then blend on high speed until completely smooth, deep green, and slightly warm to the touch, 1 to 2 minutes. It keeps in the fridge for up to 1 week.

MAKE THE SOUP:

IN a small mixing bowl, stir together the tahini, vinegar, and soy sauce until smooth and set aside.

IN a dolsot or other medium-heavy pot, heat the olive oil over medium-high heat until shimmering. Add the chilies and cook until slightly blistered, about 2 minutes, then add the garlic and ginger and cook, stirring, until fragrant, another minute or so.

ADD the white wine, let it simmer for about 30 seconds, then add the mushroom stock. Let it come to a boil, skimming any froth, then add the tahini mixture and stir well. Reduce the heat to cook at a moderate simmer and squeeze in the sundubu (or spoon in the silken tofu in four big pieces) and cook, without stirring, until they're just warmed through, about 3 minutes.

TOSS the greens in a medium mixing bowl with the dressing. Serve the stew in bowls topped with the greens.

POTATO AND PERILLA LEAF STEW

SERVES 4 TO 6

This stew gets its earthy flavor from pulverized perilla seeds, its vibrancy from licorice-y, citrus-y fresh perilla leaves, and its heat from gochugaru and gochujang. It'll be somewhat familiar to fans of gamjatang, which literally translates to "potato stew" but whose headliner is not so much the single tuber often plunked in but rather large hunks of pork neck and back. Not here. Instead the potatoes break down a bit to give the stew body, adding a comforting quality that reminds me of the much more tame but delightful baked potato soup I ate as a kid at Chili's.

   The sauce on the side, packing the vibrant and totally nontraditional punch of wasabi, is for dunking the cabbage, mushrooms, and anything else that you grab with chopsticks.

FOR THE DIPPING SAUCE

¼ cup soy sauce

2 tablespoons distilled white vinegar

1 tablespoon toasted sesame oil

1 tablespoon extra-virgin olive oil

1 teaspoon agave syrup

1 teaspoon prepared wasabi, plus more for serving

FOR THE STEW

3 ounces dried shiitake (about 10 large), soaked and trimmed (see page 234)

⅓ cup extra-virgin olive oil

1 large leek (white and light green parts only), finely chopped

A fat 3-inch knob ginger, peeled and finely chopped

3 garlic cloves, finely chopped

4 cups Mushroom Stock, homemade (page 230) or store-bought

1 pound russet potatoes, cut into 1-inch cubes

2 cups chopped drained spicy cabbage kimchi, homemade (page 14) or store-bought

½ cup thinly sliced white or yellow onion

½ cup thinly sliced scallions

2 tablespoons gochugaru (Korean chili flakes)

1 tablespoon gochujang (Korean red chili paste)

3 serrano chilies, stemmed and halved lengthwise

Kosher salt

FOR SERVING

2 cups soybean sprouts

12 large Napa cabbage leaves

½ pound chrysanthemum greens or watercress, woody bottoms trimmed, roughly chopped

2 tablespoon deulkkae-garu (dried perilla seed powder)

12 fresh perilla leaves or shiso leaves

MAKE THE DIPPING SAUCE:

MIX all the ingredients in a small mixing bowl and set aside.

MAKE THE STEW:

QUARTER the mushroom caps.

COMBINE the olive oil and leeks in a medium pot, set it over high heat, and bring it to a sizzle. Cook, stirring, until the leeks are translucent, about 2 minutes, then add the ginger and garlic and cook until fragrant but not colored, about 30 seconds.

ADD the mushroom stock, potato, and mushrooms, let it come to a simmer, and cook, covered and adjusting the heat to keep the simmer moderate, until the potatoes are so tender they begin to break apart, about 20 minutes. Remove the cover, add the kimchi, onion, scallions, gochugaru, gochujang, and chilies, and bring to a boil over high heat. Reduce the heat to cook at a moderate simmer until the onions are tender, about 10 minutes more. Season with salt.

PREP THE GARNISHES AND SERVE:

WHILE it's cooking, bring a large pot of water to a boil and salt it so it's salty but not as salty as pasta water. Fill a large mixing bowl with ice water. Add the bean sprouts to the boiling water, cook for 30 seconds, then use a skimmer to transfer them to the ice water. Next, cook the cabbage leaves in two batches, adding each batch to the boiling water and cooking until the thick white stems are tender, 1 to 2 minutes. Transfer them to the ice water, too. When it's all cool, use your hands to move the bean sprouts and cabbage leaves to a kitchen towel to drain well. Tear the cabbage leaves in half lengthwise.

LADLE the stew into bowls and top with the chrysanthemum greens. Serve the bean sprouts, cabbage leaves, deulkkae-garu, and perilla leaves on a plate for garnishing each bowl and the dipping sauce on the side with a little extra wasabi to taste.

ARMY STEW

SERVES 4

Budae-jjigae, or "army stew," was created after the Korean War, when food was relatively scarce and some resourceful cook (many accounts attribute it to a woman named Heo Gisuk) incorporated processed meat like Spam and bacon from American army bases into a spicy stew. The dish took off, and now you can find it bubbling away tableside, with blocks of instant noodles still in their wavy uncooked form, in big, wide pots in Korean restaurants and homes.

There's no meat in this one, canned or otherwise, but there are garlicky beans (baked beans are a common addition) and tahini in place of the common add-on of sliced processed cheese that melts into the broth. It's legitimate fun to pluck out the sundry bits with chopsticks—a snarl of garlic chives, a deposit of kimchi. And I especially enjoy the variety in the recipe here—the enoki mushrooms, inari, firm tofu, noodles, and rice cakes are all tender and soft in different ways. It's simple. It comes together quickly. And it's undeniably delicious.

Note: I like to char the inari over flames to give the sweet-salty ingredient another dimension of flavor. If you're up for it, set a wire rack (it might warp, so not a fancy one) directly on a stovetop burner and turn the heat to medium high. In batches if necessary, cook the inari in a single layer on the rack, flipping once, until well charred but not burnt on both sides, about 30 seconds total.

4 cups Mushroom Stock, homemade (page 230) or store-bought, or water

Two 4-ounce packages vegan instant ramyeon, including seasoning packets

1 tablespoon gochugaru (Korean chili flakes)

6 tablespoons well-stirred tahini (I love Soom)

3 tablespoons unseasoned rice vinegar

2 teaspoons soy sauce

3 tablespoons extra-virgin olive oil

4 garlic cloves, thinly sliced

One 13-ounce can red kidney beans, drained

1 teaspoon kosher salt, or more to taste

14 ounces enoki mushrooms, trimmed of ½ inch of the woody base

1 pound firm tofu, drained and cut into 1-inch cubes

2 cups Korean rice cakes—slices or sticks, soaked in cold water for 30 minutes and drained well

2 cups chopped spicy cabbage kimchi, homemade (page 14) or store-bought

1 cup crumbled roasted seaweed

1 cup drained inari

1 cup roughly chopped garlic chives or scallions

Handful mixed herbs, such as basil and perilla leaves or shiso

IN a medium mixing bowl, stir together the stock, ramyeon seasoning packets, and gochugaru. In a small mixing bowl, stir together the tahini, vinegar, and soy sauce. Set both aside.

PUT the oil and garlic in a wok or heavy skillet, set it over high heat, and let the oil sizzle. Cook until the garlic is fragrant but not colored, about 30 seconds. Stir in the beans and cook until they're warmed through, about 2 minutes. Turn off the heat. Add the salt and season with more to taste.

IN a large Dutch oven or other soup pot, arrange the beans, mushrooms, tofu, rice cakes, kimchi, seaweed, inari, and garlic chives in piles around the edges, then add the blocks of instant noodles to the center. No need to be neat about it. Pour in the stock mixture.

BRING the liquid to a boil over high heat, then boil, stirring once halfway through, until the rice cakes and noodles are cooked through, about 3 minutes. Season with salt.

DRIZZLE on the tahini mixture, sprinkle on the herbs, and serve.

MINO'S LENTIL SOUP

SERVES 4

The most requested breakfast from my son, Mino, is "soup and rice." By soup, he means this one, which I had to learn how to make after he threw down the gauntlet, telling me, "My mom makes really good lentil soup."

So a recipe from Youngmi might be the dish in this book I make the most, because, honestly, it's really good lentil soup. I like to add umami salt and pepper for a boost of complexity and to stir in coconut flakes, which get nice and chewy as they rehydrate. Mino doesn't seem to mind, though he still prefers his mom's.

1 tablespoon extra-virgin olive oil, plus more for finishing

½ cup diced (¼ inch) white or yellow onion

1 garlic clove, finely chopped

1 tablespoon tomato paste

1 cup split red lentils

1 tablespoon kosher salt, or more to taste

1 teaspoon Umami Salt and Pepper (page 231)

1 fresh bay leaf, bruised/crumbled

¼ cup unsweetened toasted coconut flakes or Smoky Coconut (page 227)

HEAT the oil in a medium pot over medium until it shimmers. Add the onion and cook, stirring, until translucent, 3 to 4 minutes, then add the garlic and tomato paste and stir until the oil takes on a deep red color, 30 seconds to 1 minute.

ADD the lentils, stir well, then add 6 cups water, salt, umami salt and pepper, and bay leaf. Raise the heat and bring the liquid to a boil, skimming off any froth. Adjust the heat to cook at a moderate simmer and cook, uncovered, stirring occasionally, until the lentils break down and the soup thickens and looks creamy, about 30 minutes. Season with salt.

MEANWHILE, if you're not using the smoky coconut, preheat the oven to 325°F.

SPREAD the coconut flakes on a small sheet pan and bake, rotating the pan halfway through, until lightly browned, 4 to 6 minutes.

SERVE in bowls, sprinkle on the coconut flakes, and drizzle on some olive oil.

SEAWEED SOUP

SERVES 6 TO 8

For many years, I was focused on each dish at my restaurants making a big impact. Practically every dish from the blistered long beans to the stir-fried peas to the chicken wings to the cold buckwheat noodles was laced with fire from dried chilies and fresh chilies, roasted and raw chilies, and mouth-numbing Sichuan peppercorns. When I ate out, I'd seek the same sorts of thrill, dare-deviling around town trying the biggest, the boldest, the hottest dishes. If I tried miyeok-guk during those days, I doubt I'd remember.

Yet as my tastes and cooking evolved, I came to appreciate more subtle flavors. And then I came to crave them. Now I go out of my way for this Korean seaweed soup, relishing the relative blandness of the broth and the slick texture of ocean vegetable miyeok, or wakame, in Japanese. The soup often comes with something chewy—mussels, brisket, or, in this case, chewy shiitake. When I make it, I only slightly amp up the classic with a little quick-pickled garlic, flavor-boosting shio kombu, and pink peppercorns for a touch of fruity heat.

FOR THE QUICK-PICKLED GARLIC

¼ cup very thinly sliced garlic

1 teaspoon granulated sugar

½ teaspoon kosher salt

2 tablespoons unseasoned rice vinegar

FOR THE DISH

1 ounce dried miyeok or wakame

1½ ounces dried shiitake (about 5 large), soaked and trimmed (see page 234)

Four 1-inch squares dasima or dashi kombu

2 tablespoons white soy sauce

1 tablespoon toasted sesame oil

1 teaspoon kosher salt

2 tablespoons shio kombu

1 tablespoon extra-virgin olive oil

1 teaspoon coarsely cracked pink peppercorns

MAKE THE PICKLED GARLIC:

PUT the garlic in a small mixing bowl, sprinkle on the sugar and salt, and toss well. Let it sit for 10 minutes. Add the garlic to a small, narrow container, stir in the vinegar, and let it pickle for 15 minutes or so before using.

MAKE THE DISH:

IN a medium mixing bowl, soak the miyeok or wakame in plenty of warm water for 20 minutes. Drain well. Cut the mushroom caps into bite-sized pieces. If using miyeok, snip it into ½-inch pieces after soaking.

COMBINE the mushrooms, miyeok, dasima, soy sauce, sesame oil, salt, and 8 cups water in a medium pot, bring it to a gentle simmer, and cook, adjusting the heat if necessary, for 15 minutes, so the flavors come together.

SERVE in bowls and add the shio kombu, olive oil, peppercorns, and as much pickled garlic (and some pickling liquid, too) as you want.

PEA LEAVES IN PUMPKIN BROTH

SERVES 4 TO 6

This one joins only a handful of early Mission Chinese dishes that have stuck around for all these years, morphing and changing as I did. Like our mapo tofu, the recipe got simpler as time went on, shedding the fussy techniques, cerebral embellishments, and other relics of my ego. Now, it's just what it was supposed to be when I first made it: really good brothy greens. The kabocha we once mandolined as a garnish is now roasted so it's earthy and sweet, and mashed up in the broth to thicken it. There's rehydrated dried bean curd, instead of house-pressed or house-smoked tofu, for its delightful chew. The charred chili paste remains. It delivers fire and umami, though who knows, by next year I might drop it, too.

Note: The greens you're after are sold under many names—pea greens, pea shoots, pea leaves, and snow pea tips. They come as short hollow stems attached to medium-sized leaves. Once you remove any woody stems and tough tendrils, the greens are tender with a pea flavor, though with only the slightest sweetness. I've found the best place to find them is at Chinese and Korean markets and some farmers markets. They're notably not the same thing as those delicate pea shoots (wispy stems with a few small leaves attached) sold near the salad greens.

½ medium kabocha (about 1½ pounds), seeds scraped out

¼ cup plus 1 tablespoon extra-virgin olive oil

¼ cup finely chopped garlic (about 12 cloves)

1 tablespoon plus 2 teaspoons kosher salt

Scant 2 teaspoons white sugar

2 teaspoons Mushroom Seasoning Powder, homemade (page 231) or store-bought

2 teaspoons soy sauce

1 pound pea greens (about 16 cups loosely packed)

3 ounces dried bean curd stick, soaked 2 hours in cold water, drained, and roughly chopped

2 tablespoons Charred Red Chili Paste (page 222), or more to taste

2 tablespoons roasted salted pumpkin seeds (pepitas)

2 tablespoons toasted pumpkin seed oil

PREHEAT the oven to 350°F.

RUB the squash all over with 1 tablespoon of the olive oil and bake, cut-side down, on a sheet pan until the flesh and skin are very soft, about 45 minutes.

COMBINE the garlic and the remaining ¼ cup olive oil in a medium pot, set it over medium-high heat, and let it sizzle. Cook, stirring, until it's fragrant, 30 seconds to 1 minute. Add the squash (there's no need to remove the skin), use a spoon to break it into smallish pieces, and turn the heat to high. Once it sizzles, cook, stirring occasionally, for a minute, then stir in 8 cups water along with the salt, sugar, mushroom seasoning powder, and soy sauce.

LET it come to a boil, skim off some of the froth, then add the pea greens in several batches, stirring after each batch to wilt. Stir in the bean curd stick. Cook at a boil, stirring occasionally, until the pea green stems are tender but with some texture, about 3 minutes. Season with salt.

TRANSFER to a large serving bowl and top with the chili paste, pumpkin seeds, and pumpkin seed oil. Serve right away.

KIM'S KABOCHA CONGEE

SERVES 4

My friend Kim frequently hosts soup parties, and this is what I always bring—because once she tried it, she wouldn't let me bring anything else. It's a riff on two of my favorite New York comfort foods—the Chinese rice porridge at Congee Village, and the lentil soup from Bereket, a beloved but now-closed Turkish spot on Houston Street where I used to go practically every night after service. The sweet, nutty roasted kabocha squash that I stir into the porridge gives it the same ruddy color as that lentil soup and the mint (fresh, in this case) and lemon give it a similar brightness.

Note: Here's a trick to prevent the congee from boiling over as it cooks because of all that starch from the rice. Take two chopsticks and set them on either side of the pot, so they create a platform for the pot's lid, then set the lid on the chopsticks.

1 cup uncooked jasmine rice

2 tablespoons Mushroom Seasoning Powder, homemade (page 231) or store-bought

1 tablespoon plus 1 teaspoon kosher salt, or more to taste

1 large kabocha (about 3 pounds), halved horizontally, seeds scraped out

2 tablespoons grapeseed or olive oil

1 heaping tablespoon Ginger-Scallion Sauce (page 225), or more to taste

¼ cup unsalted roasted pumpkin seeds (pepitas)

1 tablespoon plus 1 teaspoon pumpkin seed oil or extra-virgin olive oil

2 cups mixed herbs like mint leaves, chrysanthemum greens, and dill fronds, roughly chopped

4 lemon wedges

PREHEAT the oven to 350°F.

IN a large pot, combine the rice, mushroom seasoning powder, 1 tablespoon of the salt, and 16 cups water and bring to a boil over high heat. Reduce the heat, use chopsticks to create a vented lid (see note, above), and cook at a steady simmer, stirring after 30 minutes or so, until the grains of rice fall apart and the mixture has a slightly creamy soupy consistency, about 1 hour.

MEANWHILE, rub the squash halves all over with the grapeseed oil, season with the remaining 1 teaspoon salt, and bake, cut-sides down, on a sheet pan until the flesh and skin are very soft, 45 to 55 minutes. Scoop the flesh into a bowl, mash well with a fork, and stir in 2 cups water.

WHEN the rice porridge is ready, turn off the heat, add the squash mixture to the pot, and season with salt. Divide among bowls, then add the ginger-scallion sauce, pumpkin seeds, pumpkin seed oil, and herbs to each bowl. Serve with lemon wedges.

CHILLED TOFU IN PEANUT MILK

SERVES 4

I got hooked on peanut milk when I lived in San Francisco. Near my apartment, there was a small restaurant run by a Taiwanese couple, Jack and Margaret Chang, that sold omelets, crinkle-cut fries, veggie burgers, and, famously, peanut milk. The story goes that Jack loved peanuts but couldn't chew them because he had a dental situation, so he blended up this concoction of peanuts, water, and various spices and strained the puree to make a drink. He claimed, along with a bunch of testimonials tacked to the wall, that it solved all sorts of health issues.

I can't speak to that, but I can attest that chilled peanut milk tastes really good. Serving it with tofu delivers some of the pleasures of the cold Korean noodle soup called kong-guksu (page 126). It's light and refreshing, but also rich and luxurious, the perfect partner for some of the louder dishes in this book.

FOR THE PEANUT MILK

2 cups unsalted roasted Spanish peanuts

1 tablespoon granulated sugar

1 teaspoon kosher salt

FOR SERVING

1 pound firm tofu, drained and cut into 1-inch cubes, chilled

12 or so ice cubes

2 tablespoons Chili Oil, homemade (page 228) or store-bought

2 tablespoons thinly sliced scallions

MAKE THE PEANUT MILK:

PUT the peanuts in a medium mixing bowl, add enough water to cover by about 2 inches, and let them soak for at least 8 hours, preferably overnight.

DRAIN the peanuts and rinse under cold water. Transfer the nuts to a blender along with 6 cups fresh water, the sugar, and salt. Blend until smooth. Strain the mixture through a fine-mesh sieve or a nut milk bag, pressing the solids to extract as much liquid as possible. Refrigerate until chilled.

IT keeps in the fridge for up to 1 week. Stir before you use it.

SERVE THE DISH:

DIVIDE the tofu among bowls, then serve with the peanut milk, ice cubes, chili oil, and scallions.

NOODLES AND
DUMPLINGS

MATCHA PHỞ

SERVES 4

For years at Mission, we served an awesome riff on the ginger-scallion noodles I used to have for breakfast at the sadly-now-closed Hing Lung in San Francisco's Chinatown. We mixed ginger-scallion sauce and mushroom seasoning powder with a little boiling water and tossed in fresh Japanese ramen noodles. On top, we added sliced cucumber and radish, a little hoisin (which is what I'd do at Hing Lung since each table had a bottle and I tend to like things sweet), and a dusting of matcha for its vivid color and savory, unexpected umami.

Even though my original inspiration was pretty clear, whenever I ate the noodles, they reminded me of something else, too, flavors I couldn't quite put my finger on. The breakfast-specific memories, the noodles, the umami from matcha, the crunch of the vegetables we added on top—it was the phở at Phở Liên Hòa, in Oklahoma City!

So here's the next iteration of one of my favorite Mission dishes. It's a little brothier than the original and has sriracha and hoisin stirred in—a no-no when carefully cooked phở broth is involved, but a yes-yes here. To finish, there's sharp, licorice-y Thai basil, crunchy bean sprouts, and plenty of matcha.

¼ cup Ginger-Scallion Sauce (page 225)

¼ cup hoisin sauce

1 tablespoon plus 1 teaspoon Mushroom Seasoning Powder, homemade (page 231) or store-bought

1 tablespoon plus 1 teaspoon sriracha, or more to taste

Kosher salt

12 ounces dried sweet potato starch noodles (dangmyeon), soaked in cold water for 30 minutes and drained well, or 1 pound narrow flat rice noodles (bánh phở)

2 teaspoons matcha powder

2 cups (6 ounces) bean sprouts

1 cup lightly packed Thai basil leaves, roughly chopped cilantro, or a mixture

BRING at least 5 quarts water to a boil in a large pot.

WHEN the water boils, scoop 6 cups into a medium pot. Add the ginger-scallion sauce, hoisin sauce, mushroom seasoning powder, and sriracha, stir well, and season with salt. Cover to keep warm. Add the noodles to the boiling water and cook, stirring once, until they're cooked the way you like, according to the instructions on the package. Drain them well.

DIVIDE the broth among four serving bowls, then divide the noodles among them. Put the matcha in a sifter or fine-mesh strainer and sift it (if using the strainer, knock it gently against your palm) evenly over each bowl. Top with the bean sprouts and herbs and serve hot.

LEMON PEPPER GLASS NOODLES

SERVES 4

In culinary school, I was taught to fear lemon pith. Whenever I zested citrus, I'd carve off the peel and meticulously remove the white part, which we were told was unappealingly bitter. After graduation, one of my early gigs was at a sushi bar where they served a roll topped with paper thin slices of lemon—peel, pith, and all—and I immediately fell for its explosive flavor.

Here, chopped whole lemon provides tart-bright-bitter pops among slick, chewy glass noodles, plus there's black bean sauce for salty umami and a ton of chives for freshness. Lots of freshly ground pepper adds a nice burn and the combo with the citrus evokes the lemon pepper seasoning from my Oklahoma family spice rack.

8 ounces dried wide glass noodles (made from sweet potato or "green bean")

2 tablespoons extra-virgin olive oil

1 scallion, trimmed, halved lengthwise, and cut into 2-inch pieces

⅓ cup dry white wine

2 tablespoons Black Bean Sauce (page 226)

2 teaspoons cracked black pepper

1½ lemons, quartered, seeded, and sliced ¼ inch thick

1 cup roughly chopped chives

1 teaspoon toasted sesame seeds

SOAK the noodles in a few inches of warm water for 30 minutes, to soften them. Gently pull them apart, if necessary, then drain well.

PUT the oil and scallions in a wok or heavy skillet, set it over high heat, and let the oil sizzle. Cook until the scallions turn brown, about 1 minute, then add the noodles and stir until they soften further and become translucent, 20 seconds or so.

STIR in the white wine, black bean sauce, and black pepper, let it come to a boil, and cook, stirring occasionally, until the noodles are tender and chewy and the sauce has reduced to glaze the noodles, about 1 minute.

TAKE the wok of the heat, then add the lemon, chives, and sesame seeds and toss well. Serve right away.

SOMYEON IN ICED SOY MILK

SERVES 4

The more I eat Korean food, the more I appreciate dishes that aren't as bold or spicy as the ones that first caught my interest. Nowadays, I'm just as likely to seek out kong-guksu, noodles in chilled soy milk soup, as I am to order fiery bibim-naengmyeon. Its flavors are quiet, but it still makes a big impact: the creamy, lightly seasoned broth is served ice-cubes-floating-in-there cold and topped with raw cucumber and tomato, so it's super-refreshing. I add an unconventional sprinkle of shio kombu—kelp that's been cooked with soy sauce, dried, and cut into little strips dense with salt and umami.

FOR THE SOY MILK

1 pound dried yellow soybeans, picked over

⅓ cup raw cashews

1 tablespoon toasted sesame seeds

FOR THE DISH

Ice cubes for ice bath, plus 2 cups ice cubes for serving

1 pound dried somyeon

5 ounces Persian or Japanese cucumbers, cut into matchsticks (about 1 cup)

1 cup halved cherry tomatoes

1 cup thinly sliced fresh shiso or perilla leaves

1 tablespoon shio kombu

Flaky sea salt

MAKE THE SOY MILK:

IN a large mixing bowl or jar, combine the soybeans and enough water to cover by a few inches. Cover and let them soak at room temperature for at least 10 hours or up to 24 hours. When they're ready, they'll split easily when gently squeezed.

DRAIN the soybeans well, put them in a medium pot, and add enough fresh water to cover by about 2 inches. Bring to a boil, then reduce the heat to simmer gently, partially covered with a lid, until slightly softened but still quite firm, about 20 minutes. Let them cool slightly in the liquid, about 10 minutes.

FINALLY, drain the soybeans, reserving ½ cup of the cooking liquid. In two batches, blend the soybeans, cashews, and sesame seeds along with the reserved liquid and 6 cups of fresh water. Blend until very smooth, up to 4 minutes, depending on your blender.

TRANSFER to an airtight container and keep in the fridge until well chilled, at least 4 hours or up to 1 week.

MAKE THE DISH:

BRING a large pot of water to a boil. Fill a large mixing bowl with water and a bunch of ice and set it aside. Add the noodles to the boiling water, stir well, and cook, stirring occasionally because somyeon like to stick together, until tender but slightly chewy, about 3 minutes. Drain the noodles, then add them to the icy water and stir until they're chilled. Drain again really well.

DIVIDE the noodles among four bowls. Pour on 1½ cups soy milk per bowl, add the cucumbers, cherry tomatoes, shiso leaves, shio kombu, a sprinkle of flaky salt, and the remaining ice cubes and serve.

KNIFE-CUT NOODLES IN SHIITAKE AND SQUASH SOUP

SERVES 4

While the contents of a pot of kal-guksu vary, the homey soup—so crowded with vegetables and starch it reminds me of Italian minestrone or Southern-style chicken and dumplings—always features the thick, hand-cut noodles that give it its name. Even if you've never made noodles yourself, you can make these. Then as the dead-simple dough rests, you throw together the soup, simmering summer squash until it's soft and juicy and kabocha until it breaks down slightly to thicken the broth. Those sweet-vegetable flavors are offset by the acidity of kimchi, not a typical addition to the dish itself but a common sight on the side.

FOR THE NOODLE DOUGH

3 cups all-purpose flour

1½ teaspoons kosher salt

FOR THE DISH

12 cups Mushroom Stock, homemade (page 230) or store-bought

2 cups slices (½-inch-thick half-moons) zucchini

2 cups slices (½-inch-thick half-moons) summer squash

2 cups cubed (1 inch) kabocha squash

1 cup chopped spicy cabbage kimchi, homemade (page 14) or store-bought

2 tablespoons kosher salt, plus more for the boiling water

1 teaspoon freshly ground black pepper

1 tablespoon toasted sesame oil

1 cup crumbled roasted seaweed

MAKE THE NOODLE DOUGH:

MIX the flour and salt in a medium mixing bowl. Make a well in the middle, and in a slow, steady stream, pour ¾ cup plus 2 tablespoons water into the well as you stir with a fork. Use your hands to bring the dough together. If necessary, in order to incorporate all the flour into the dough, add more water, a teaspoon at a time, and work it in.

KNEAD the dough until it's smooth and springs back slightly when you poke it, about 10 minutes. Transfer it to a bowl, cover with a damp towel, and let it rest at room temperature for 30 minutes.

MAKE THE DISH:

WHILE the dough rests, make the soup. Combine the stock, zucchini, summer squash, kabocha, kimchi, 2 tablespoons salt, and the pepper in a large, heavy pot and bring to a simmer over high heat. Reduce the heat to cook at a moderate simmer and cook, skimming any froth, until the kabocha is tender, about 20 minutes. Season with salt. Turn off the heat, stir in the sesame oil, and cover to keep warm.

BRING a large pot of water to a boil and season with salt until it's slightly salty. Lightly flour a clean work surface and a rolling pin. Use the rolling pin to roll out the dough to a 12 x 6-inch rectangle that's ¼ to ⅛ inch thick. Fold the dough like a letter. Cut the dough in half the short way, then stack the halves and slice the short way to make noodles that are somewhere between ¼ inch and ⅛ inch thick. Gently unfurl them.

BOIL the noodles until tender but still chewy, 3 to 5 minutes. Drain well. Put the noodles in four bowls, ladle on the hot soup, and top with the seaweed.

HAND-TORN NOODLES IN HOT PEPPER BROTH

SERVES 4

The noodles in sujebi are special. Common in Korean home cooking, they're super-rustic, made from a simple dough that you tear by hand and drop, noodle by irregular noodle, directly into bubbling broths. They cook up slick and chewy with plump edges, adding heft and even more textural variety to this fiery soup crowded with tofu, kimchi, and shiitakes.

FOR THE NOODLE DOUGH

2 cups all-purpose flour

1 teaspoon kosher salt

FOR THE BROTH

4 dried shiitake, soaked and trimmed (see page 234)

1 pound firm tofu, drained and cut into 1-inch cubes

2 cups chopped spicy cabbage kimchi, homemade (page 14) or store-bought

¼ cup soy sauce

2 tablespoons gochujang (Korean red chili paste)

2 tablespoons gochugaru (Korean chili flakes)

1 tablespoon Mushroom Seasoning Powder, homemade (page 231) or store-bought

1 teaspoon kosher salt, or more to taste

MAKE THE NOODLE DOUGH:

MIX the flour and salt in a medium mixing bowl. Make a well in the middle, and in a slow, steady stream, pour ½ cup plus 2 tablespoons water into the well as you stir with a fork. Use your hands to bring the dough together. If necessary, in order to incorporate all the flour into the dough, add more water, a teaspoon at a time, and work it in.

KNEAD the dough until it's smooth and springs back slightly when you poke it, about 10 minutes. Transfer it to a bowl, cover with a damp towel, and let it rest at room temperature for 30 minutes.

MAKE THE BROTH:

WHILE the dough rests, make the broth. Quarter the mushroom caps.

COMBINE the mushrooms and the rest of broth ingredients along with 4 quarts water in a medium pot and bring to a boil over high heat. Partially cover with a lid, reduce the heat, and cook, stirring occasionally and skimming off any froth, at a simmer for 20 minutes, just so the flavors come together. Season with salt. Turn off the heat and cover to keep warm.

WHEN the dough has sufficiently rested, bring the broth to a boil. Holding the ball of dough in one hand, use the other to tear off then stretch a small piece of the dough to make an irregular matchbook-size noodle with edges that are slightly thicker than the middle (for guidance, see the images below). Drop it into the broth. Continue with the rest of the dough, stirring gently after adding every three or four noodles.

ONCE you've added them all, lower the heat to cook at a moderate simmer and simmer until the noodles are slippery, cooked through, and still chewy, about 2 minutes from when you added the last one. Serve in bowls.

COLD BUCKWHEAT NOODLES WITH RADISH WATER KIMCHI BROTH

SERVES 4

The liquid from radish water kimchi (page 13) is so delicious that cooks use it to flavor broth for cold noodles, in particular the super-chewy buckwheat kind called naengmyeon. In fact, they're so chewy people usually cut the long noodles with scissors to make the task of eating them a little easier. Chewy noodles are fun, but so is seasoning the dish yourself with the hot mustard (I've also been served wasabi) and vinegar served alongside. I like it when the dish starts out quiet, then by the time you take your last bite, the intensity of the mustard makes you sneeze.

Note: If you don't make or can't find radish water kimchi, you can substitute any non-spicy radish or cabbage kimchi.

FOR THE MUSTARD

2 tablespoons hot mustard powder

1 tablespoon unseasoned rice vinegar

¼ teaspoon Mushroom Seasoning Powder, homemade (page 231) or store-bought

FOR THE BROTH

8 cups Mushroom Stock, homemade (page 230) or store-bought

2 cups peeled, sliced (½-inch half-moons) Korean radish or daikon

½ cup soy sauce

1 cup chopped Radish Water Kimchi, homemade (page 13) or store-bought (see note), plus 1 cup of its liquid

Kosher salt

FOR THE DISH

24 ounces fresh or frozen naengmyeon (buckwheat noodles), or 20 ounces dried naengmyeon

10 ounces Persian or Japanese cucumbers, cut into matchsticks

1 tablespoon gochugaru (Korean chili flakes)

1 cup thinly sliced or crumbled roasted seaweed

2 cups ice cubes

MAKE THE MUSTARD:

IN a small serving bowl, combine 3 tablespoons water and mustard powder, stir well, and let sit for 5 minutes, to mellow the mustard. Stir in the vinegar and mushroom seasoning powder and set aside.

MAKE THE BROTH:

COMBINE the stock, radish, and soy sauce in a large heavy pot and bring to a boil over high heat. Cover, reduce the heat, and cook at a moderate simmer until the radish is juicy-tender, about 12 minutes. Uncover the pot, add the kimchi and kimchi liquid, and raise the heat to bring to a boil. Once it boils, turn off the heat and let the broth cool completely. Season with salt.

KEEP it in the fridge until it's cold, at least 2 hours or up to 8 hours. Longer than that and its bright flavor suffers.

MAKE THE DISH:

BRING a large pot of water to a boil. Fill a large mixing bowl with water and a bunch of ice and set it aside. Add the noodles to the boiling water, stir well, and cook until fully tender but still very chewy, about 4 minutes. Drain the noodles, then add them to the icy water and stir until they're chilled. Drain again really well.

DIVIDE the noodles among four bowls, pour on the chilled kimchi broth, and add the cucumbers, gochugaru, and seaweed. Add the ice cubes and serve.

COLD BUCKWHEAT NOODLES WITH DRAGON FRUIT ICE

SERVES 4

One of the countless ways Korean food excites me is that it employs extreme temperature—whether it's serving food in the ripping-hot stone pots called dolsot or frozen bowls. I remember the chef world—myself included—nerding out when Noma served squid with broccoli in a vessel made entirely of ice, only to find myself, a few weeks later, eating naengmyeon out of one in Flushing, Queens.

There's no ice bowl required for this dish, though I do take a page from a restaurant I went to in Seoul where they put the chilled broth into a slushy machine. My at-home version uses a savory-sweet granita to top the cold, super-chewy buckwheat noodles in a spicy dressing. The addition of dragon fruit powder is 100-percent not traditional and 95-percent optional, but it does add a little sweetness and an absolutely spectacular neon pink color. Got that trick from Starbucks.

4 cups Mushroom Stock, homemade (page 230) or store-bought, chilled

½ cup apple juice

2 tablespoons freeze-dried dragon fruit powder

1 tablespoon Korean or Japanese apple vinegar

24 ounces fresh or frozen naengmyeon (buckwheat noodles), or 20 ounces dried naengmyeon

1 large Asian pear, peeled, cored, and roughly chopped

½ cup agave syrup or maple syrup

3 tablespoons gochugaru (Korean chili flakes)

2 tablespoons gochujang (Korean red chili paste)

2 tablespoons Korean or Japanese apple vinegar

1 tablespoon soy sauce

One ¼-inch-thick slice peeled ginger

1 large garlic clove

1 teaspoon kosher salt

1 teaspoon toasted sesame oil

10 ounces Persian or Japanese cucumbers, cut into matchsticks (2 cups)

1 cup drained chopped spicy cabbage kimchi, homemade (page 14) or store-bought

MAKE THE DRAGON FRUIT ICE:

COMBINE the stock, apple juice, dragon fruit powder, and vinegar in a medium mixing bowl and stir well. Pour into a 9 x 7-inch metal baking dish or another container where the mixture is about 2 inches deep. Freeze, using a fork to scrape the ice every 30 minutes, until it's fluffy and fully frozen, about 3½ hours.

COVERED, it keeps in the freezer for up to 2 days. You might need to stir and scrape it to turn it back into fluffy shaved ice.

MAKE THE DISH:

PREPARE a large bowl of ice water and set aside. Bring a large pot of water to a boil. Add the noodles, stir well, and cook until fully tender but still very chewy, about 4 minutes or according to the package instructions. Drain, then add the noodles to the ice water and stir until they're chilled. Drain again really well and use scissors to snip them into manageable lengths.

COMBINE the Asian pear, agave, gochugaru, gochujang, vinegar, soy sauce, ginger, garlic, salt, and sesame oil in a blender and blend until smooth. Combine the sauce and noodles in a large mixing bowl and toss to coat well.

SERVE in bowls, garnish with the cucumber and kimchi, and top with the dragon fruit ice.

BLACK BEAN SAUCE NOODLES

SERVES 6

When I was in Korea, Youngmi's mom was eager for me to try Korean-Chinese food. Like so many countries, Korea has restaurants that specialize in a hybrid cuisine that blends local and Chinese flavors and techniques. The result is always worth eating.

One especially tasty staple in the Korean-Chinese food canon is jjajangmyeon (a Korean-ified pronunciation of the Mandarin zhájiàngmiàn), wheat noodles topped with black bean sauce. First, chunjang (Korean fermented black bean paste) gets toasted in plenty of fat, so it feels really decadent, and mixed with vegetables like onion, zucchini, and potato, so it feels kind of healthy, too. Try it and see why it's one of the go-to takeout dishes in Korea and so popular it spawned an instant version. I love eating it with fresh jjajangmyeon, a thin Korean wheat noodle that sometimes has the word "udon" on the label, or boiled instant noodles.

FOR THE SAUCE

2 ounces dried shiitake (about 8 large), soaked and trimmed (see page 234)

1 cup extra-virgin olive oil

1 cup (3 ounces) small clusters of maitake or oyster mushrooms

1 cup (3 ounces) sliced (¼-inch-thick half-moons) king trumpet mushrooms

¼ cup Korean black bean paste

2 tablespoons finely chopped garlic

1 tablespoon toasted sesame oil

1 cup diced (1 inch) peeled Korean radish or daikon

1 cup diced (1 inch) white or yellow onion

1 cup diced (1 inch) russet potato

1 cup diced (1 inch) zucchini

1 tablespoon Mushroom Seasoning Powder, homemade (page 231) or store-bought

1 cup finely crumbled firm tofu

1 cup finely chopped drained inari

2 tablespoons potato starch

FOR THE DISH

2 tablespoons Korean black bean paste

2 tablespoons unseasoned rice vinegar

¾ cup very thinly sliced white and yellow onion

30 to 36 ounces fresh jjajangmyeon or 6 packages instant ramyeon noodles (without the seasoning packets)

1 generous cup fresh perilla leaves or shiso leaves, torn

1½ cups sliced (¼-inch-thick half-moons) yellow pickled radish

8 ounces Persian or Japanese cucumbers, cut into matchsticks

MAKE THE SAUCE:

FINELY chop the mushroom caps.

HEAT the olive oil in a large Dutch oven over medium-high until it shimmers. Add the dried and fresh mushrooms and cook, stirring, until golden brown, 8 to 10 minutes. Stir in the bean paste, garlic, and sesame oil and cook until the bean paste and garlic are very fragrant, about 30 seconds.

ADD 3 cups water, the radish, onion, potato, zucchini, and mushroom seasoning powder, let it come to a boil, then reduce the heat to cook at a moderate simmer until the potatoes are tender, about 10 minutes. Stir in the tofu and inari. In a small mixing bowl, stir the potato starch with 2 tablespoons water until smooth, then a tablespoon at a time, add the mixture to the pot, stirring vigorously during and after each addition. Let it return to a bubble and cook until the liquid thickens, 20 seconds or so. Turn off the heat and cover to keep warm.

MAKE THE DISH:

IN a small mixing bowl, mix together the black bean paste and vinegar and set it aside. Fill a medium mixing bowl with ice water, add the onions, and let them soak.

BRING a large pot of water to a boil. Cook the noodles in the boiling water until fully tender but still nice and chewy, 2 to 4 minutes. Drain the noodles well. Drain the onions, too.

PUT the noodles in bowls, ladle on the sauce, and serve with the vinegar mixture and the perilla leaves, pickled radish, and cucumbers for garnishing each bowl.

CHILLY GREEN CHILI NOODLES

SERVES 4

A tart paste of charred chilies electrifies noodles, bringing enough heat that you'll be grateful that they're served chilled. I really like that sensation of spicy and cold, which you also see in the fiery buckwheat noodles on page 134. The result is exhilarating and refreshing, just the thing to break you out of a kitchen rut. Lots of fresh herbs lifts the dish and the freshness tempts you back, despite all the fire, for another bite.

The chewy, slick fresh semolina noodles, which I learned how to make from chef Paolo Laboa, are relatively low effort and will surprise anyone who thinks they can't make pasta at home. If you're not up for making them, 1¼ pounds of fresh Japanese ramen or fresh spaghetti works great here.

FOR THE NOODLE DOUGH

2½ cups semolina rimacinata (very fine semolina flour), plus extra for dusting

FOR THE DISH

Kosher salt

2 cups Charred Green Chili Paste (page 222)

½ cup extra-virgin olive oil

Sichuan peppercorn powder

2 cups mixed herbs, such as Thai basil leaves, mint leaves, and cilantro

1 lemon

MAKE THE NOODLE DOUGH:

SIFT the semolina flour onto a clean work surface, form a pile, and make a well in the middle. In a thin, steady stream, pour about ½ cup lukewarm water into the well while stirring with a fork to incorporate the liquid into the flour as it's added. Bring the dough together, then add ¼ cup lukewarm water and use your hands to bring the rough dough together, making sure you've incorporated all the flour.

KNEAD the dough until it's smooth and springs back slightly when you poke it, about 5 minutes. Transfer it to a bowl, cover, and let it rest at room temperature for 30 minutes.

CUT the dough into two equal-ish pieces. Dust a work surface with semolina flour and use a rolling pin to roll out each piece to a thickness somewhere between ¼ inch and ⅛ inch. Dust each one with a little more semolina flour. Fold each one into thirds and cut into noodles that are somewhere between ¼ inch and ⅛ inch thick. Gently toss to separate the noodles and dust once more with a little semolina flour.

TO freeze the noodles, divide them into four tangles, put them on a plate or tray, and freeze, uncovered, until solid. Transfer to freezer bags, forcing out the air as you close them. There's no need to thaw before cooking.

MAKE THE DISH:

BRING a large pot of generously salted water to a boil. Fill a large mixing bowl with water and a bunch of ice and set it aside. Add the noodles to the boiling water and cook to al dente, 3 to 5 minutes. Drain the noodles, then add them to the icy water and stir until they're chilled. Drain again really well.

DUMP out the water and wipe the large mixing bowl dry. Add the noodles, chili paste, olive oil, and salt to taste, and toss really well. Divide among plates, garnish with the Sichuan peppercorn powder and herbs, then grate on the zest of the lemon. Cut the lemon into wedges and serve with the noodles.

PASTA POMODORO

SERVES 4 TO 6

I make this sauce once a week, at least. When it came time to write down the recipe, I came up with only four ingredients and I was sure I was forgetting something. Nope. It's that simple and it comes together quickly—garlic and basil briefly fried in olive oil, top-quality canned tomatoes just brought to a simmer—not for convenience but because that's how it keeps its vibrancy.

Note: To find great San Marzano canned tomatoes, look for the "DOP" on the label, which means they are what they claim to be. I use the La Carmela brand when I can, though there are lots of good ones out there.

Kosher salt

¼ cup extra-virgin olive oil, plus more for finishing

1 garlic clove, smashed and peeled

12 or so Italian basil leaves, plus another 12 or so for finishing

One 28-ounce can whole San Marzano (DOP) tomatoes

A double batch of fresh semolina noodles (see page 142) or 26 ounces dried fettuccine

BRING a large pot of salty water to a boil.

MEANWHILE, combine the oil and garlic in a large skillet, set it over medium-high heat, and let it start to sizzle. Tilt the skillet away from you, so the garlic fries over the heat in the oil that pools at the edge, and cook until golden brown, 30 seconds to 1 minute. Over medium-high heat again, stir in the basil and cook until it's almost crispy, 10 to 20 seconds.

TURN off the heat (this will help avoid splattering), add the tomatoes and 2 teaspoons salt, then turn the heat back to medium. Let the mixture come to a full simmer, stirring and breaking up the tomatoes, though I like it pretty chunky. Take it off the heat and season with salt.

COOK the noodles in the boiling water until fully cooked but still nice and chewy, 2 to 4 minutes. Drain the noodles well, then add them to the skillet with the sauce and toss well.

SERVE in bowls with the rest of the basil and a drizzle of oil.

SOMYEON IN SEAWEED BROTH

SERVES 4

I came to Itaewon for Parmesan, but ended up leaving with a deep affection for somyeon in seaweed broth. I was in Korea for my wedding, and I'd volunteered to cook at a church. The congregants had requested Italian food, and my hosts were excited to take me to the Itaewon district, close to a US Army base, to an international grocery store. On the way home, I spotted a vendor with a stall set up beneath a stairwell. My hosts warned me off, saying it was old people food, so of course, I had to head over.

The small bowl I got brought me back to my job at Blowfish Sushi, in San Francisco, where the chefs converged on the cold station between shifts to gulp down a concoction of Japanese somen (similar to Korean somyeon) and seaweed salad doused with miso soup, and to Olive Garden, since the narrow noodles made me think of the angel hair pasta I enjoyed enveloped in alfredo sauce. It was better than anything I made for the churchgoers.

When I make something similar at home, I bulk it up with some extra vegetables and serve sauce on the side for dunking the noodles and other goodies.

2 tablespoons dried miyeok or wakame

2 tablespoons dried goji berries

2 teaspoons dried tot or hijiki

6 ounces dried shiitake (about 20 large), soaked and trimmed (see page 234)

4 cups peeled, diced (1 inch) Korean radish or daikon

1 teaspoon kosher salt

1 teaspoon soy sauce

1 tablespoon Mushroom Seasoning Powder, homemade (page 231) or store-bought

12 ounces dried somyeon

½ pound yellow summer squash, sliced lengthwise into thin ribbons (a mandoline helps here!)

2 tablespoons toasted sesame oil, plus 1 tablespoon for finishing

1 cup thinly sliced or crumbled roasted seaweed

1 tablespoon gochugaru (Korean chili flakes)

1 tablespoon thinly sliced scallions or chives

IN a medium mixing bowl, combine the miyeok, goji berries, and tot, cover by 1 inch with warm water, and let soak for 20 minutes. Drain them well. Quarter the mushroom caps.

COMBINE the mushrooms, radish, salt, soy sauce, mushroom seasoning powder, and 6 cups water in a medium pot. Bring it to a boil over high heat, then reduce the heat and cook at a simmer, partially covered, until the radish is juicy-tender, about 15 minutes. Turn off the heat and keep hot.

BRING a large pot of water to a boil. Add the noodles to the boiling water, stir well, and cook, stirring occasionally because somyeon like to stick together, until tender but slightly chewy, about 5 minutes.

DRAIN the noodles well and divide them among four bowls, then add the squash, miyeok, goji berries, tot, and 2 tablespoons sesame oil. Ladle the hot soup into each bowl, then add the roasted seaweed, gochugaru, scallions, and remaining 1 tablespoon sesame oil. Serve right away.

SOMYEON SALAD WITH SESAME, YUZU, AND SHISO

SERVES 6

When I'm hungry and it's hot out, I throw together this quick noodle salad, really cold somyeon tossed with creamy, tart dressing and topped with whatever I find after raiding my fridge and pantry. You can go in so many directions—swapping in mint and basil for the shiso, frisee or arugula for the mixed greens, sauteed mushrooms for the sweet, chewy inari.

FOR THE DRESSING

1 tablespoon yuzu or lemon juice

1½ teaspoons white (shiro) miso

¼ cup plus 2 tablespoons unseasoned rice vinegar

¼ cup well-stirred tahini (I love Soom)

FOR THE DISH

1 pound dried somyeon

2 cups sliced (¼ inch) drained inari (about 20)

3 cups lightly packed mixed greens

10 ounces Persian or Japanese cucumbers, cut into matchsticks (about 2 cups)

2 cups sliced (¼-inch strips) fresh shiso

¼ cup toasted sesame seeds

MAKE THE DRESSING:

IN a medium mixing bowl, combine the yuzu juice and miso and stir until smooth, then add the vinegar and tahini and stir well.

MAKE THE DISH:

BRING a large pot of water to a boil. Fill a large mixing bowl with water and a bunch of ice and set it aside. Add the noodles to the boiling water, stir well, and cook, stirring occasionally because somyeon like to stick together, until tender but slightly chewy, about 3 minutes. Drain the noodles, then add them to the icy water and stir until they're chilled. Drain again really well.

COMBINE the noodles and inari in a large mixing bowl, add the dressing, and toss well. Add the mixed greens, toss gently, and serve in bowls topped with the cucumbers, shiso, and sesame seeds.

Making fresh yuba at the Hodo Soy factory in California

CUMIN-FLAVOR TOFU SKIN

SERVES 4

I still remember the first time I was at a Chinese restaurant and saw cumin called out on the menu. I was new to San Francisco, and friends took me to a restaurant called Old Mandarin Islamic, specifically for a dish called Extremely Hot Pepper. Yet while I came to have my tongue scalded, I left with a new obsession: "cumin-flavored" dishes.

Until then, I had mainly associated the spice with the Tex-Mex I had in Oklahoma. When our cumin lamb came, the sheer amount of the spice surprised me. We're not talking the pinch I was used to tasting, but a ton, both in powder form and whole seeds. Other than that, the stir-fry was simple: the meat, some onion and green chili (cooked just briefly so they retained their crisp textures), and cilantro. There was no sauce per se, just the cumin-heavy seasoning clinging to everything.

That's what you'll find here in a dish inspired by northwestern Chinese cooking—from Xinjiang and Shaanxi—but minus the lamb, of course. Instead, I use Japanese yuba, the skin that forms when soy milk is heated to make tofu, sliced so it eats like a chewy noodle. If you can't find it, sub in 2½ ounces dried "bean curd stick," soaked for 2 hours in cold water, then drained and cut into 2-inch pieces.

5 ounces yuba (tofu skins), preferably the Hodo Soy brand

2 tablespoons Shaoxing wine, dry sake, or white wine

2 tablespoons soy sauce

1 teaspoon granulated sugar

1 teaspoon Mushroom Seasoning Powder, homemade (page 231) or store-bought

½ teaspoon kosher salt

1 tablespoon roughly chopped garlic

1 teaspoon cumin seeds, plus 1 teaspoon for garnish

1 teaspoon ground cumin, plus 1 teaspoon for garnish

1 tablespoon olive oil

1 medium long green chili, halved lengthwise and cut into 1-inch pieces

½ medium red onion, sliced into thin half-moons

A handful roughly chopped cilantro

Chili Oil, homemade (page 228) or store-bought

GENTLY unfold the yuba, pull apart the sheets, and slice into long 1-inch wide ribbons. Set them aside. Combine the Shaoxing wine, soy sauce, sugar, mushroom seasoning powder, salt, and 3 tablespoons water in a small mixing bowl, stir well, and set aside.

COMBINE the garlic, cumin seeds, ground cumin, and olive oil in the skillet and set it over medium-high heat. When the garlic starts to sizzle, give it a stir and cook until you can smell the garlic but it hasn't browned, 30 to 45 seconds.

ADD the Shaoxing wine mixture and cook, swirling the pan, for 5 seconds. Add the chili and onion, stir for 10 seconds, then add the yuba and cook, tossing frequently, until the yuba is coated in sauce, about 1 minute. You might need to add a tablespoon or two of water to help the sauce coat the yuba, though there shouldn't be any sauciness in the pan.

TRANSFER to a platter, top with the cilantro and the whole and ground cumin, then drizzle on some chili oil.

KIMCHI DUMPLINGS

MAKES 24 DUMPLINGS

In Seoul I spend a lot of time at Kimbob Nara, a cheerful, modest storefront with an enormous menu of Korean standards. For me it was an education on some of the dishes Koreans eat all the time but that I'd never heard of. Of course, they served the restaurant's namesake, kimbob (or gimbap), rice crammed with humble ingredients like egg, pickled radish, and carrots, then wrapped in dried seaweed and sliced into pucks, which I'd had many times in New York. But they also made a soup of glass noodles and bulgogi, sweet porridge made from winter squash, and ra-bokki, a merging of ramyeon (instant noodles) and tteok-bokki (see page 190) that comes with an optional slice of processed cheese melted on top.

    I tried something new every time, but my order always included the kimchi mandu, dumplings filled with crunchy chopped spicy cabbage kimchi mixed with garlic chives, tofu, and sweet potato noodles. They're so good and light I could eat two dozen in a sitting. In other words, this recipe will serve four of your friends or one me.

FOR THE FILLING

3 ounces dried sweet potato starch noodles (dangmyeon), soaked in cold water for 30 minutes and drained well

¼ pound firm tofu

½ cup finely chopped spicy cabbage kimchi, homemade (page 14) or store-bought

¼ cup thinly sliced garlic chives

1½ teaspoons gochugaru (Korean chili flakes)

1½ teaspoons toasted sesame oil

1½ teaspoons Mushroom Seasoning Powder, homemade (page 231) or store-bought

FOR THE DUMPLINGS

24 square dumpling wrappers

3 tablespoons extra-virgin olive oil

1 tablespoon toasted sesame oil

No-Cook Hot Sauce (page 229)

MAKE THE FILLING:

BRING a large pot of water to a boil. Add the noodles and boil, stirring occasionally, until they're tender but still chewy, about 8 minutes. Drain well and use scissors to snip them into 1-inch pieces.

CUT the tofu in half horizontally and press it between paper towels or a clean kitchen towel to remove excess liquid. Give the kimchi a gentle squeeze to drain off its liquid. Crumble the tofu into a medium mixing bowl, then add the noodles, kimchi, chives, gochugaru, sesame oil, and mushroom seasoning powder and mix well.

FORM THE DUMPLINGS:

PUT a heaping teaspoon of the kimchi mixture in the center of each dumpling wrapper. Dip two fingers in water and rub the edges of the wrapper. Fold the wrapper corner to corner to make a triangle, then firmly press the edges together so they stick together. Keep them in the fridge—in a single layer or with layers separated by parchment paper—until you're ready to cook them, up to 12 hours.

COOK THE DUMPLINGS:

COMBINE the olive oil and sesame oil in a small mixing bowl and stir well. Bring a large pot of water to a boil. Add the dumplings and cook for 2 minutes. Taste a dumpling to be sure the wrapper is cooked. Drain the dumplings, drizzle with the sesame oil mixture and some hot sauce, and serve right away.

CILANTRO-TAPIOCA POT STICKERS

MAKES 24 DUMPLINGS

Like a lot of my cooking, these dumplings are a sort of mash-up of food I love that other people made. In this case, one of those foods is the magical cilantro dumplings at Dim Sum Go Go (see page 174) and the other is a creation of Iñaki Aizpitarte. The French-Basque chef behind the game-changing Le Chateaubriand, in Paris, served a perfect snack at the restaurant's little sister next door, Le Dauphin. A riff on a Brazilian dish of fried cubes of cheese and tapioca flour, his contained a little surprise: tapioca pearls.

I couldn't stop thinking about the experience of biting through a shatteringly crisp exterior, then getting the joy of those tiny, slippery, chewy pearls. So when Iñaki came in to eat at Mission, I served him these pan-fried dumplings, which I think make a similar impact.

I only pan-fry them at home when I'm feeling ambitious or when Mino wants dumplings. Otherwise, I boil them, and you should feel free to as well. Also optional, but really satisfying and delicious, is making the lace (aka the skirt) you see in the photo, a web of delicate crispiness that connects the dumplings. It's easy, I promise. Hang in there, though: like making pancakes or crepes, your second attempt will be better than your first.

FOR THE DIPPING SAUCE

¼ cup Chinkiang vinegar

2-inch knob ginger, peeled and cut into very thin matchsticks

FOR THE FILLING

1 bunch cilantro, stem bottoms trimmed

½ cup small tapioca pearls

1 teaspoon Mushroom Seasoning Powder, homemade (page 231) or store-bought

½ teaspoon kosher salt

½ teaspoon granulated sugar

24 circular dumpling wrappers

2 tablespoons cornstarch

2 tablespoons grapeseed or another neutral oil, plus 1½ teaspoons for the pan

MAKE THE DIPPING SAUCE:

IN a small serving bowl, combine the vinegar and ginger and stir. Set the bowl aside while you make the dumplings.

MAKE THE FILLING:

BRING a large pot of water to a boil. Add the cilantro to the boiling water and cook for 2 minutes. Use tongs to transfer the cilantro to a colander, leaving the water in the pot. Rinse the cilantro well under cold water, then drain well. Use your hands to squeeze the cilantro to remove any excess water. Chop the cilantro into ⅛- to ¼-inch pieces.

BRING the pot of water back to a boil. Add the tapioca pearls and cook for 1 minute. Turn the heat to medium, cover the pot, and cook at a steady simmer until the tapioca pearls are no longer opaque in the center, about 10 minutes. Drain, rinse well under cold water, and drain well. Set aside.

IN a medium mixing bowl, combine the tapioca pearls, cilantro, mushroom seasoning powder, salt, and sugar and stir well.

FORM THE DUMPLINGS:

FILL a small bowl of water. Grab a dumpling wrapper from the pile in the packet and put it on your work surface. Dip two fingers in the water and rub the edges of the wrapper.

SPOON 1 tablespoon of the filling in the center of the wrapper. Fold the wrapper in half over the filling and pinch together the edges of the wrapper at one of the corners. Next, make a small fold in the edge of the wrapper facing you (and toward the direction of the pinched corner) to make a pleat. Pinch the pleated edge against the opposite edge so they adhere, then continue to make as few as four or as many as eight pleats, depending on the size of the pleats and your skill at this process. Finally, pinch the opposite corner closed, then give the entire pleated edge of the dumpling another good pinch to ensure it's completely and firmly sealed. Put the dumpling on the tray and repeat with the rest of the wrappers and filling. Keep them in a single layer with a little space between them so they don't stick together and cover with plastic wrap or a damp kitchen towel.

KEEP them in the fridge until you're ready to cook them, up to 12 hours.

COOK THE DUMPLINGS:

PUT the cornstarch in a medium mixing bowl, then pour in 2 cups water, in a thin stream at first while whisking to avoid clumps. Whisk in 2 tablespoons of the oil the same way.

COOK the dumplings in three batches: Set a 10-inch nonstick skillet over medium-high heat for a minute or two, so it's hot. Add ½ teaspoon of the remaining oil, give it a quick swirl in the skillet, then arrange eight dumplings in the skillet in a pinwheel formation so they're touching slightly. Cook until the bottoms of the dumplings are light golden, 1 to 2 minutes. Give the cornstarch mixture a brief whisk, then add ½ cup to the skillet so it coats the entire bottom of the pan, cover with a tight-fitting lid, and cook for 5 minutes (no peeking!). Remove the lid and continue to cook until the liquid has completely evaporated and what's left is a lacy, golden brown "skirt," 5 to 7 minutes more.

TURN off the heat and leave the dumplings in the pan for 30 seconds so the skirt sets. To remove them, invert a plate onto the skillet, carefully hold it in place with one hand, then quickly invert both plate and skillet so the dumplings are skirt-side up on the plate.

SERVE the first batch with the sauce for dipping. Cook the next two batches in the same way, serving them as soon as they're done.

LUNG SHAN'S VEGAN DELIGHT

SERVES 4

Never say never. Because I did and I was embarrassingly wrong. Way back when I came on board Anthony Myint's Mission Street Food, we made all sorts of weird, cool stuff. And I don't think I ever stopped complaining about these dumplings, which cropped up on the Lung Shan part of the menu and served as an option for vegans who came in. I was deep in fancy-chef mode at the time, and I couldn't deal with the fact that on a menu full of thrills, we were offering mushroom dumplings in miso soup.

They were really good, sure. But I just kept thinking that they could be so much more. Anthony kept telling me that not every last dish had to be some mind-warping culinary revelation. I grudgingly caved, but vowed never to make them again.

So, ten years later, now that pretty much all of my ego has been wrung out of me and I've come to enjoy simpler, quieter cooking, I'm sharing them with you. When I called to tell Anthony, he laughed. He was right the whole time.

FOR THE DUMPLINGS

¼ cup extra-virgin olive oil

2 cups thinly sliced stemmed shiitake (about 5 ounces)

2 cups thinly sliced stemmed button mushrooms (about 5 ounces)

½ teaspoon Mushroom Seasoning Powder, homemade (page 231) or store-bought

¼ teaspoon kosher salt

1 tablespoon white (shiro) miso

16 square wonton wrappers

FOR THE DISH

4 cups Mushroom Stock, homemade (page 230) or store-bought

1 tablespoon white (shiro) miso

2 scallions, trimmed and thinly sliced

MAKE THE DUMPLINGS:

HEAT the oil in a wide heavy skillet over high heat until it's really hot but before it smokes. Add the mushrooms, stir well, and cook, stirring occasionally, until they're all nice and soft (a little color is fine, but not necessary), about 4 minutes.

STIR in the mushroom seasoning powder and salt and cook for another 30 seconds or so. Transfer the mushrooms to a mixing bowl, add the miso, and mix well (the miso will be a little clumpy, so you really want to make sure it's evenly distributed).

TO make each dumpling, put a tablespoon or so of the mushroom mixture in the center of a wonton wrapper. Dip your finger in some water and rub it onto the border of the wrapper. Fold the wrapper corner to corner to make a triangle, then firmly press the edges together so they adhere. They keep for up to a day in the fridge. Keep them in a single layer with a little space between them so they don't stick together and cover with plastic wrap or a damp kitchen towel.

MAKE THE DISH:

IN a small pot, bring the mushroom stock to a boil. Put the miso in a small bowl, scoop a couple tablespoons of the hot broth into the bowl, and stir until smooth. Turn off the heat and stir in the miso mixture. Cover and keep warm.

BRING a large pot of water to a boil. Carefully add the dumplings and cook for 1½ minutes. Taste a dumpling to be sure the wrapper is cooked. Drain the dumplings, then divide them among four bowls. Pour the broth over the dumplings and sprinkle on the scallions. Serve right away.

RICE

SCORCHED RICE

SERVES 1 TO 4

One afternoon in a food market in Seoul, I spent a good hour watching a vendor who specialized in scorched rice. Operating many wide pots at once, she boiled rice until it was cooked but still looked a bit wet, then used a spoon to rapidly and methodically spread the grains across the bottom and up the sides of the pot. After a while, she used a spatula to free the rice from the pan, removing a concave disc with a crackling golden brown base that was also somehow still supple enough to fold in half without snapping before she tucked it into to-go bags.

Her stall, I'd later learn, was devoted to nurungji, the Korean name for scorched rice. I'd always enjoyed scraping the grains from the bottom of dolsot-bibimbap (page 180), and I'd been to Korean homes where friends would dislodge the crackly bottom from pots of simple white rice. Nurungji then joined the running list in my head of words that cultures around the world use for this delightful consequence of rice cookery—*tahdig* in Iran, *socarrat* in Spain, *okoge* in Japan.

At home, I've started making an amateur's version of those big crispy-chewy rice discs I saw in the market. And you can, too. Sprinkle on some sugar and snack away. Or serve it with Charred Chili Paste (page 222) and Whipped Garlic Sauce (page 220) for dipping, or try it with Tiger Salad (page 86), using pieces of the scorched rice to grab the dressed greens.

¾ cup short-grain white rice

SOAK the rice in cold water for 20 minutes, then drain well.

HEAT a 10-inch nonstick or well-seasoned cast-iron skillet over high heat, let it get hot, then add ¾ cup water. Let it boil, stir in the rice, then cook uncovered until the water has completely evaporated, about 3 minutes.

STARTING from the center of the rice, use a metal spoon to both spread and firmly press the rice to form a thin layer that covers the bottom and about 1 inch up the sides of the skillet. Continue to cook over high heat, without messing with it, until the edges start to pull away from the skillet and you can lift the whole thing from the pan in one piece, 8 to 10 minutes. Turn off the heat.

SLIDE a spatula under the rice bowl to remove it, running a spoon along the edges to loosen them if necessary. Serve crispy side up, warm or at room temperature.

FRAGRANT CHILI FRIED RICE WITH HERBS

SERVES 4

There was a Korean restaurant in San Francisco that I went to all the time but won't name, because part of its appeal was that it stayed open way past the city's 2 a.m. last call, pouring diners soju from teapots for another few hours. The place served a lot of drinking food, much of it spicier than anything I'd had then or have had since. This one dish called fire chicken would come out on a sizzling platter, fajita-style, and it was beyond hot. I couldn't get enough.

Basically, they would puree chilies and other seasonings, then pour the sauce over the chicken on the platter. When it hit that hot-hot surface, it hissed and spit and let loose a cloud of fragrant, tear-inducing vapor. At Mission, I wanted to do that—to serve something brutally spicy *and* something that came out on a sizzling platter, so that once the first order hit the dining room, everyone would take notice and start asking for it. Ultimately, I applied this flamboyant presentation to fried rice, a typically mild-mannered dish made unruly by the intense chili sauce and balanced by loads of fresh herbs.

If you don't have a fajita platter at home, which I also do not, a cast-iron skillet works just as well. Just make sure when you pour on the sauce, your windows are open and everyone's prepared for the excitement.

RICE

MAKE THE SAUCE

½ cup thinly sliced serrano chilies (about 6)

2 tablespoons soy sauce

1 tablespoon granulated sugar

½ teaspoon kosher salt

½ teaspoon gochugaru (Korean chili flakes)

FOR THE DISH

¼ cup plus 1 tablespoon extra-virgin olive oil

2 tablespoons thinly sliced garlic

12 drained oil-cured Calabrian chilies, stemmed and halved lengthwise

4 cups freshly cooked jasmine rice

1 tablespoon Mushroom Seasoning Powder, homemade (page 231) or store-bought

½ cup sliced (½-inch half-moons) red onions

½ cup sliced (½ inch) seeded red, yellow, or orange bell peppers

Big handful torn mixed herbs like basil, mint, and perilla leaves or shiso leaves

1 cup thinly sliced or crumbled roasted seaweed

MAKE THE SAUCE:

COMBINE all the ingredients with 2 tablespoons water in a blender and blend on high speed until very smooth.

MAKE THE DISH:

COMBINE ¼ cup of the oil and the garlic in a large skillet, set it over high heat, and let it start to sizzle. Cook, stirring, until the garlic is fragrant but not colored, about 30 seconds. Stir in the Calabrian chilies and turn off the heat. Fold in the rice to coat it in the oil.

COMBINE the mushroom seasoning powder and 1 tablespoon warm water in a bowl, stir to dissolve, and add the mixture to the skillet. Keep folding to gently mix well and eliminate any rice clumps. Turn the heat back to high and cook, stirring gently, just until hot all the way through. Turn off the heat and set aside.

SET a large cast-iron skillet or fajita platter over medium heat for 3 to 5 minutes, so it gets really hot. Toss the onions and peppers with the remaining 1 tablespoon olive oil in a small mixing bowl. When the skillet is hot, add the onions and peppers in a single layer and watch them sizzle and smoke. Add the rice on top of the vegetables in a more or less even layer, turn off the heat, then pour the sauce evenly over the rice.

SPRINKLE on the herbs and roasted seaweed and serve.

PINEAPPLE-KIMCHI FRIED RICE

SERVES 4

Kimchi fried rice is a common sight in Korea and in my apartment. Pineapple fried rice is my Thai takeout go-to. One day at Mission, we were trying out a quick-fermented kimchi made with pineapple and suddenly realized we could use it to make a mash-up of the two fried rices. OK, there are actually three represented here, because the sesame seeds and garlic-and-(vegan)-butter combo is ripped from the Benihana classic.

If you haven't made the pineapple kimchi, no stress: Mix equal parts chopped aged cabbage kimchi and crushed fresh pineapple. It'll still taste great.

2 tablespoons extra-virgin olive oil

½ cup thinly sliced scallions

1 large garlic clove, thinly sliced

2 cups drained Pineapple Kimchi (page 7)

1 tablespoon unsalted vegan butter

4 cups freshly cooked jasmine rice

1 tablespoon toasted sesame seeds

1½ teaspoons soy sauce

1 teaspoon Umami Salt and Pepper (page 231)

Kosher salt

1 cup thinly sliced or crumbled roasted seaweed

4 pinches gochugaru (Korean chili flakes)

PUT the oil, scallions, and garlic in a wok or heavy skillet, set it over high heat, and let the oil sizzle. Cook until the scallions and garlic are fragrant but not colored, about 2 minutes. Add the kimchi and vegan butter and cook, stirring and tossing, until the kimchi is warmed through, about 1 minute. Turn off the heat.

ADD the rice, sesame seeds, and soy sauce and use a wooden spoon or flexible spatula to gently stir, breaking up any clumps but not smashing the grains. In a small mixing bowl, combine the umami salt and pepper and 1 tablespoon warm water, stir to dissolve, and add the mixture to the skillet.

TURN the heat to high and cook just until it's hot through, 30 seconds to 1 minute. Season with salt. Sprinkle on the seaweed and gochugaru and serve.

PORTOBELLO JERKY FRIED RICE

SERVES 4

How I came up with this dish was actually a mystery to me until I sat down to explain it for this book. Then I realized it's a composite of flavors from my go-to order from Somtum Der, a restaurant on Avenue A in Manhattan imported from Bangkok that specializes in northeastern Thai food.

They do a really good, simple mushroom fried rice, so I always get that, plus one of several aromatic soups finished with sawtooth herb—a leaf with serrated edges used in Thailand as well as in Puerto Rican and Dominican food, where it goes by *recao* or *culantro*—and larb, the protein-heavy "salad" made with shallots and more sawtooth. My rice preparation is like a fever-dream version of that meal.

But the potato chips? At the time we put the fried rice on the menu at Mission, I'd often come home from work late and make myself José Andrés's ingenious tweak on the Spanish tortilla, in which potato chips take the place of fresh potatoes. Here, they offer a similar satisfaction, slowly rehydrating as you eat and turning chewy.

FOR THE JERKY

2 tablespoons extra-virgin olive oil

2 tablespoons soy sauce

1 tablespoon granulated sugar

1 tablespoon Mushroom Seasoning Powder, homemade (page 231) or store-bought

1 tablespoon smoked paprika

1 tablespoon ground black pepper

2 pounds portobello mushrooms, stems removed, cut into ½-inch-thick slices

FOR THE DISH

2 teaspoons Umami Salt and Pepper (page 231)

1 teaspoon granulated sugar

¼ cup extra-virgin olive oil

2 garlic cloves, thinly sliced

4 cups freshly cooked jasmine rice

2 cups coarsely crumbled salted potato chips

½ cup sliced (¼ inch) sawtooth herb

½ cup very thinly sliced red onion

MAKE THE JERKY:

PREHEAT the oven to 250°F.

IN a large mixing bowl, combine the oil, soy sauce, sugar, mushroom seasoning powder, smoked paprika, and black pepper and stir well. Add the mushrooms and toss gently until evenly coated, taking care not to break them. Spread the mushrooms on two large parchment paper–lined sheet pans in a single layer, leaving a little space between them.

BAKE until the mushrooms look deep brown and shriveled, their surface is dry, and they're chewy, like jerky, about 2 hours.

LET them cool completely, then store in an airtight container in the fridge for up to 4 days.

MAKE THE DISH:

IN a small mixing bowl, combine the umami salt and pepper, sugar, and 1 tablespoon warm water and stir to dissolve. Chop enough mushroom jerky into ½-inch pieces to give you 2 cups.

COMBINE the oil and garlic in a large nonstick skillet, set it over medium-high heat, and let the oil sizzle. Cook, swirling occasionally, until the garlic turns golden brown, about 45 seconds. Add the mushroom jerky, stir to coat in the oil, then turn off the heat.

ADD the rice and stir gently, breaking up any clumps but not smashing the grains. Stir in the sugar mixture, turn the heat to high, and cook, stirring occasionally, just until it's hot through, 30 seconds to 1 minute. Add the chips and give it all one more good toss.

TRANSFER to plates and garnish with the sawtooth herb and onions. Serve right away.

UME-SHISO FRIED RICE

SERVES 4

At EN Japanese Brasserie in Manhattan, which also inspired the Scallion-Miso Dip for vegetables (page 224), they make a great garlicky fried rice heaped with slivered roasted nori and shiso, the jagged-edged herb common in Japanese cooking and in a world of its own in terms of flavor. As someone who has long finished his sushi meals with ume-shiso maki, I'm not used to eating nori and shiso together without umeboshi. The salty and sour dried pickled fruit (usually translated as a "plum," but actually a member of the apricot family) delivers a tart wallop to this dish, which I consider an homage to both the rice and the roll. The umeboshi and shiso amplify each other and make this light, bright, and perfect for spring and summer meals.

¼ cup extra-virgin olive oil

2 garlic cloves, thinly sliced

2 tablespoons Ginger-Scallion Sauce (page 225)

2 tablespoons umeboshi paste

2 teaspoons Mushroom Seasoning Powder, homemade (page 231) or store-bought

4 cups freshly cooked jasmine rice

½ cup coarsely crumbled roasted seaweed, plus a handful for garnish

14 or so fresh shiso leaves, sliced (¼ inch)

COMBINE the oil and garlic in a large nonstick skillet, set it over medium-high heat, and cook, swirling occasionally, until it smells toasty and turns golden brown, about 2 minutes. Turn off the heat, then add the ginger-scallion sauce and umeboshi paste and stir, breaking up the umeboshi a bit. Combine the mushroom seasoning powder and 1 tablespoon warm water in a bowl, stir to dissolve, and add the mixture to the skillet.

ADD the rice and use a wooden spoon or flexible spatula to gently stir, breaking up any clumps but not smashing the grains. Add the roasted seaweed, stir well, then turn the heat to high and cook just until it's hot through, 30 seconds or so.

TRANSFER to a serving plate and top with the shiso and handful of roasted seaweed. Serve right away.

...nt Week!
...FEBRUARY 7TH
...CH & DINNER
♥ $20.21 ♥
YOUR CHOICE OF 1 APPETIZE...
+ SIDE OF ...

ETIZER OPTIONS
CUCUMBERS W/ TINGLY
                GRANO...
AN KIMCHI
EAR MUSHROOM S...
N WAFFLE FR...
XXX WINGS

FRAGRANT FRIED RICE WITH CHARRED BAMBOO AND HOJICHA

SERVES 4

Smoky and bright, this is one of my favorites, though it's as far from classic as can be. I take soy sauce–marinated menma, the juicy-crunchy bamboo shoots that are a common sight in bowls of Japanese ramen, and char them so they taste a little smoky. A little powdered hojicha (roasted green tea) brings more smoky fragrance, while lemon enters the picture to take the whole thing in a different direction. The citrus shows up in two bracing forms—as chewy peel-and-all slivers throughout the rice and as a peel-and-all puree with salt, chilies, and olive oil for a creamy dollop on top.

Note: Strict vegans, take note: Check the shoyu menma ingredients, because some are flavored with the help of katsuobushi (the dried fish used for dashi stock).

1 pound (2 cups packed) drained shoyu menma (soy sauce–marinated bamboo shoots)

1 tablespoon extra-virgin olive oil

Heaping ¼ teaspoon freshly ground black pepper

½ lemon, stem nub trimmed

2 teaspoons Mushroom Seasoning Powder, homemade (page 231) or store-bought

2 teaspoons granulated sugar

½ teaspoon kosher salt

2 tablespoons extra-virgin olive oil

4 cups freshly cooked jasmine rice

1 teaspoon powdered hojicha (roasted green tea)

1 teaspoon flaky sea salt, preferably smoked Maldon

¼ cup Lemon Kosho (page 219), or more to taste

MAKE THE CHARRED BAMBOO:

HEAT a large cast-iron skillet over high heat until it's almost smoking, about 5 minutes. Meanwhile, in a medium mixing bowl, toss the menma with the oil and pepper.

COOK the menma in batches, so you don't crowd the skillet: Add it to the skillet in a single layer, reduce the heat to medium-high, and cook, stirring to flip once but otherwise not messing with it, until both sides have spots of black char, 2 to 3 minutes per side. Transfer each batch to a plate.

MAKE THE DISH:

QUARTER the lemons lengthwise, flick out the seeds, then slice them all—peel, pith, and flesh—crosswise into ⅛-inch-thick pieces. Give it a rough chop and set it aside. In a small mixing bowl, combine the mushroom seasoning powder, sugar, salt, and 1 tablespoon warm water and stir to dissolve.

HEAT a large skillet over high heat, then add the oil and let it smoke lightly. Add the bamboo shoots and chopped lemon and cook, stirring, for 15 seconds or so. Turn off the heat, add the rice, and use a wooden spoon or flexible spatula to gently stir to coat it in the oil, breaking up any clumps but not smashing the grains.

STIR in the mushroom seasoning mixture, turn the heat back to high, and cook, stirring occasionally, just until it's all hot through, 30 seconds to 1 minute.

TRANSFER the fried rice to a serving plate (or pack it into a bowl, then invert onto a plate to make a cool dome shape). Sprinkle on the powdered hojicha and salt. Spoon on the lemon kosho and serve right away.

DIM SUM GO GO FRIED RICE

SERVES 4

I'm pretty sure I first ordered the Chinese parsley dumplings at Dim Sum Go Go, on East Broadway in Manhattan and a few blocks away from the old Mission, because I was curious what Chinese parsley was. Turns out it's cilantro, but in a way I wasn't used to eating it. Instead of a little of the herb raw as garnish, here it was steamed and there was lots packed into each translucent wrapper along with what I'd wager is little more than salt, sugar, and MSG. Cooking had transformed it, rounding its sharp, bright edge and making it something entirely new to me.

That flavor is on display in this vibrant green fried rice, to which I also add parsley for its vibrant green color and as a little inside joke I share mainly with myself. On the side I serve slivered ginger doused with black vinegar, the same mixture Dim Sum Go Go gives you with the dumplings.

FOR THE PARSLEY OIL

½ bunch flat-leaf parsley, trimmed and roughly chopped (1 cup packed)

¼ cup extra-virgin olive oil

⅛ teaspoon kosher salt

FOR THE DISH

2 medium bunches cilantro, bottom couple inches trimmed, plus 1 cup packed roughly chopped cilantro

¼ cup Chinkiang vinegar

1-inch knob ginger, peeled and cut into very thin matchsticks

1½ teaspoons Mushroom Seasoning Powder, homemade (page 231) or store-bought

½ teaspoon kosher salt

½ teaspoon granulated sugar

2 scallions, trimmed

2 tablespoons extra-virgin olive oil

4 cups freshly cooked jasmine rice

MAKE THE PARSLEY OIL:

COMBINE all the ingredients in a blender and pulse until the parsley is more or less submerged in the oil, then blend on high speed until pretty smooth, about 45 seconds. Stop blending, scrape down the sides, and blend again until the oil is deep green and slightly warm to the touch, about 45 seconds more. Refrigerate it to cool it down, then use right away or store in the fridge for up to 1 week.

BRING a medium pot of water to a boil. Prepare a big bowl of ice water. Add the cilantro to the boiling water, cook for 5 seconds, then use a strainer to transfer it to the ice water. When it's cool, drain well, and use your hands to firmly squeeze out as much liquid as you can. Roughly chop the cilantro and set it aside.

IN a small serving bowl, combine the vinegar and ginger and stir. In a small mixing bowl, combine the mushroom seasoning powder, salt, sugar, and 1 tablespoon warm water and stir to dissolve. Set both bowls aside.

PUT the scallions on a work surface and use the flat of a chef's knife blade to firmly whack the whites to smash them. Thinly slice the scallions. Combine the scallions and oil in a large nonstick skillet, set it over medium-high heat, and let the oil sizzle. Cook, stirring occasionally, until the scallions are dark brown and crispy, about 2 minutes.

TURN off the heat, add the rice, and use a wooden spoon or flexible spatula to gently stir to coat it in the oil, breaking up any clumps but not smashing the grains. Stir in the sugar mixture, the blanched cilantro, and 2 tablespoons of the parsley puree. Turn the heat to high and cook, stirring occasionally, just until it's hot through, about 30 seconds.

SERVE in bowls topped with the cilantro. Serve the vinegar mixture on the side, so people can season their bowls.

GOLDEN FRIED RICE

SERVES 4

The key to this vegan version of golden fried rice is enoki mushroom floss. Slow roasted so it concentrates to make a slightly chewy umami bomb, it's a mollusk-free stand-in for the scallop floss common to my favorite renditions. Like those versions, this one also has a touch of curry powder, which adds flavor and golden color without relying on egg yolk that coats the grains in the classic. R&G Lounge in San Francisco makes a spicy version I just love, so I use Thai chilies here. The flax seeds on top contribute a nice bit of texture.

FOR THE MUSHROOM FLOSS

2 teaspoons Mushroom Seasoning Powder, homemade (page 231) or store-bought

1 teaspoon Japanese curry powder

½ teaspoon granulated sugar

½ teaspoon kosher salt

1 tablespoon extra-virgin olive oil

14 ounces enoki mushrooms, bottom 1 inch trimmed

FOR THE DISH

2 tablespoons extra-virgin olive oil

2 tablespoons thinly sliced fresh red Thai bird chilies

1½ teaspoons finely chopped garlic

4 cups freshly cooked jasmine rice

2 tablespoons finely chopped pickled sushi ginger

2 tablespoons yellow or green chives

1 tablespoon golden or brown flax seeds

1 tablespoon toasted sesame seeds

MAKE THE MUSHROOM FLOSS:

PREHEAT the oven to 250°F.

GRIND the mushroom seasoning powder, curry powder, sugar, and salt in a spice grinder to a fine powder. In a medium mixing bowl, combine 1 teaspoon of the powder and the oil and stir well. Add the mushrooms and toss to coat well. Reserve the remaining powder for later.

SPREAD the mushrooms on two large parchment paper–lined sheet pans in a more or less single layer. Bake until the mushrooms have shriveled to half their size and they're chewy, like jerky, 40 to 45 minutes. Let them cool, then fairly finely chop them.

MAKE THE DISH:

IN a small mixing bowl, combine the remaining mushroom seasoning powder mixture and 1 tablespoon warm water and stir to dissolve. Heat the oil in a large heavy skillet over medium-high heat until it shimmers. Stir in the chilies and garlic and cook until fragrant but not colored, about 30 seconds.

TURN off the heat and add the rice, pickled ginger, mushroom seasoning powder mixture, and mushroom floss, then use a wooden spoon or flexible spatula to gently stir to coat the rice in the oil and seasonings, breaking up any clumps but not smashing the grains. Turn the heat back to high and cook, stirring occasionally, just until it's hot through, 30 seconds to 1 minute.

SERVE in bowls topped with the chives, flax seeds, and sesame seeds.

DOLSOT-BIBIMBAP WITH GRAPEFRUIT GOCHUJANG

SERVES 4

Aside from barbecue, bibimbap (literally "mixed rice") is probably the entry point to Korean food for most non-Koreans. It was for me. It's easy to love, an assortment of light, simple vegetable dishes arranged in little piles on warm rice. You sauce it with a gochujang-based mixture that's super-savory, a bit sweet, and slightly spicy, then mix it up. Dolsot-bibimbap is just the dish served in a mega-hot stone pot (I use a cast-iron pan at my place), which gives the rice on the bottom this incredible crunch. At home, you can eat it with whatever you want on top. Lots of Koreans use any leftover banchan in their fridge, a great way to make bibimbap an everyday part of your eating.

This recipe provides a streamlined way to start more or less from scratch, with a nice collection of simple banchan. On top, I recommend a little riff on the classic sauce that features juicy segments of tart-bitter grapefruit as well as cashew cream or creamy garlic sauce to give this vegan version some richness.

⅓ cup dried tot or hijiki

2 tablespoons granulated sugar

2 tablespoons soy sauce

1 medium zucchini (about 9 ounces), cut into thin matchsticks

Kosher salt

2 medium carrots (about 7 ounces total), peeled and cut into thin matchsticks

6 large Napa cabbage leaves

12 ounces baby spinach

1 tablespoon extra-virgin olive oil

1½ ounces dried shiitake (about 5 large), soaked and trimmed (see page 234), sliced ¼ inch thick

1 cup roughly chopped gosari (Korean fern shoots), rinsed

½ teaspoon toasted sesame oil

FOR THE DISH

3 tablespoons toasted sesame oil

6 cups freshly cooked short-grain white rice

1 cup finely chopped spicy cabbage kimchi, homemade (page 14) or store-bought

¼ cup Cashew Cream (page 227) or Whipped Garlic Sauce (page 220)

½ cup Grapefruit Gochujang (page 223)

1 teaspoon toasted sesame seeds

PREP THE DISH:

PUT the tot in a medium mixing bowl, cover with an inch of warm water, and let soak for 20 minutes. Drain well and transfer back to the mixing bowl. Combine the sugar, soy sauce, and 2 tablespoons water in a small pan, set it over medium heat, and cook just until the sugar dissolves. Pour it over the tot, stir well, and let it sit for at least 10 minutes. In a medium mixing bowl, combine the zucchini and ¾ teaspoon salt, toss well, and let sit for 10 minutes. Gently squeeze the zucchini to drain off the liquid and set aside.

BRING a large pot of water to a boil and salt it so it's salty but not as salty as pasta water. Fill a large mixing bowl with ice water.

ADD the carrots to the boiling water, cook for 10 seconds, then use a skimmer to transfer them to the ice water. Use your hands to move the carrots to another kitchen towel to drain well. Add the cabbage leaves to the boiling water and cook until the thick white stems are tender, about 45 seconds. Transfer them to the ice water, too. Use your hands to move the cabbage leaves to a kitchen towel to drain well. Chop the cabbage leaves into 1-inch pieces. Add the spinach to the boiling water, stir, and cook for 5 seconds or so. Drain well and transfer to the ice water. When it's cold, drain the spinach and use your hands to transfer it to a clean kitchen towel, wrap it tightly, and squeeze out as much water as physically possible. Set aside.

HEAT the olive oil in a large skillet over high heat until it shimmers. Add the mushrooms, spread them out in an even layer, and cook, without stirring, until golden brown on the bottom, about 2 minutes. Stir well and keep cooking over high heat, stirring every minute or so, until they're evenly golden brown, 1 to 2 minutes more. Turn off the heat, stir in ⅛ teaspoon salt, and set aside.

IN a small mixing bowl, toss the gosari with the sesame oil and set aside.

SERVE THE DISH:

HEAT a large cast-iron skillet over medium heat for 5 minutes. Add the sesame oil, swirl to coat the bottom, then add the rice, gently flattening the pile to form an even layer. With the heat still on, arrange all the vegetables—mushrooms, tot, zucchini, carrot, cabbage, spinach, and kimchi—on the rice in piles. I like to start around the outside and work toward the middle. By this time, the rice on the bottom should have a nice crust. If so, turn off the heat. If not, give it another minute.

DOLLOP on the cashew cream or garlic sauce and the gochujang, sprinkle on the sesame seeds, then bring it to the table. Stir just before serving, making sure you scrape up any crunchy bits of rice stuck to the skillet.

BARLEY RICE SALAD

SERVES 4

The moment I land in Seoul, I get hungry, because I know that once I escape Incheon International I'm heading straight to Gwangjang Market, not for blood sausage or skewers of fried fish paste but for bori-bap. My favorite stall is run by a woman who sells a metal bowl of hot steamed barley topped with your pick from the heaps of prepared shoots, greens, pickles, and other goodies laid out on her table, which often change seasonally. She splashes the bori-bap with doenjang-laced broth, adds a little gochujang and a little doenjang, then hands it over for you to stir and, if you're me, scarf it down in approximately fifteen seconds before ordering another helping.

When I make it at home, I'll often use straight-up barley or primarily barley with some white rice mixed in. Some stalls do half and half, so it's really up to you. Go the extra mile and serve it with small bowls of Quick Doenjang Stew (page 93) on the side.

FOR THE SAUCE

¼ cup doenjang

2 tablespoons finely chopped yellow or white onion

1 tablespoon gochujang (Korean red chili paste)

1 tablespoon toasted sesame seeds

2 teaspoons Korean rice syrup, agave syrup, or maple syrup

2 teaspoons toasted sesame oil

1 scallion, trimmed and finely chopped

1 garlic clove, finely chopped

FOR THE PREP

2½ cups uncooked Korean pressed barley or pearled barley

Kosher salt

12 ounces zucchini (2 medium), cut into thin matchsticks

2 cups soybean sprouts

1 teaspoon toasted sesame oil

12 ounces baby spinach

¼ cup extra-virgin olive oil

1 pound beech mushrooms, trimmed and pulled into small clusters

FOR THE DISH

2 cups roughly chopped gosari (Korean fern shoots), rinsed, or blanched julienned snow peas

2 cups finely chopped spicy cabbage kimchi, homemade (page 14) or store-bought

2 cups drained Bánh Mì Pickles (page 37)

8 cups torn (into bite-sized pieces) tender lettuces

MAKE THE SAUCE:

MIX all the sauce ingredients in a small mixing bowl until smooth.

PREP THE DISH:

BRING a large pot of water to a boil, add the barley, and boil until tender with a slight chew, about 15 minutes for pressed barley and about 25 minutes for pearled barley. Drain well and set aside.

RINSE out the pot, fill it with water, and bring it back to a boil. Salt it so it's salty but not as salty as pasta water. Fill a large mixing bowl with ice water.

IN a medium mixing bowl, combine the zucchini and 1 teaspoon salt, toss well, and let sit for 10 minutes. Gently squeeze the zucchini to drain off the liquid and set aside.

ADD the bean sprouts to the boiling water, cook for 10 seconds, then use a skimmer to transfer them to the ice water. Use your hands to move the bean sprouts to another kitchen towel to drain well. Transfer the bean sprouts to a small mixing bowl, add the sesame oil and a pinch of salt, and toss well. Add the spinach to the boiling water, stir, and cook for 5 seconds or so. Drain well and transfer to the ice water. When it's cold, drain the spinach and use your hands to transfer it to a clean kitchen towel, wrap it tightly, and squeeze out as much water as possible. Set aside.

HEAT the olive oil in a large skillet over high heat until it shimmers. Add the mushrooms, spread them out in an even layer, and cook, without stirring, until golden brown on the bottom, about 2 minutes. Stir well and keep cooking over high heat, stirring every minute or so, until they're evenly golden brown, about 2 minutes more. Turn off the heat, stir in 1 teaspoon salt, and set aside.

SERVE THE DISH:

SERVE the barley in bowls garnished with the zucchini, bean sprouts, spinach, mushrooms, gosari, kimchi, pickles, and lettuce. Spoon 1 tablespoon of the sauce over each bowl (or more if you'd like) and serve.

MULTIGRAIN RICE

MAKES ABOUT 5½ CUPS

When I ordered rice in Korea, what came was often more than just rice. Sometimes there was barley, too, or mung beans or a mixture of rice types, all providing different textures and flavors. It's called japgok-bap (basically, "multigrain rice"), and it's delicious and pretty and feels extra healthy. I add quinoa to the mix, because I love its pop.

Here's a great combo: This rice with pickled perilla leaves (see page 41) on the side.

½ cup short-grain brown rice

2 tablespoons pearled barley

2 tablespoons short-grain sweet (glutinous) rice

1 tablespoon green mung beans

1 cup short-grain white rice

2 tablespoons quinoa

2 tablespoons forbidden (black) rice

COMBINE the brown rice, barley, sweet rice, and mung beans in a mixing bowl, cover by a few inches with water, and let soak at least 2 hours at room temperature or in the fridge overnight. Drain well.

COMBINE the brown rice mixture and the white rice, quinoa, and forbidden rice in a large mesh strainer, rinse under cold running water until the water runs clear, and drain really well. Transfer to an electric rice cooker or a medium pot and add 2 cups fresh water.

IF you're using the rice cooker, you know what to do. If you're using a pot, bring to a full boil on your hottest burner, then cover and transfer it to your lowest burner set to very low heat. Make sure the simmer is nice and gentle, then cook, covered and without peeking inside, for 20 minutes. Take the pot off the heat and let the rice sit covered in the pot for 10 minutes.

FLUFF and serve.

THE WALROD SPECIAL

SERVES 4

When I first met Jim Walrod, the late design legend, I had no idea how particular he was about what he ate. Because I'd watched him eat the hottest dishes on our menu, coughing, sweating, and using all the napkins on the table, but you know, gracefully. After his fourth or so visit, though, some mutual friends clued me in: Jim didn't do spicy and he didn't do green garnishes, and at the time that described basically everything on my menu. He had just been so stoked to hang that he powered through.

So I came up with the Jim Walrod Special, which, because Jim was a creature of habit, he had twice a week, at least. It's a simple sweet, salty, chewy stir-fry of rice cakes and inari age, tofu slices deep fried then simmered with soy and sugar sold at Japanese grocery stores. No heat, no Sichuan peppercorn, no cilantro. I love making this dish, because it centers me. It reminds me why I started cooking in the first place. Not for ego. But to make people I love happy.

2 tablespoons soy sauce

1 tablespoon granulated sugar

1 teaspoons Mushroom Seasoning Powder, homemade (page 231) or store-bought

½ cup extra-virgin olive oil

4 cups sliced Korean rice cakes (about 24 ounces), soaked in cold water for 30 minutes and drained well

2 tablespoons thinly sliced garlic

2 cups drained inari, halved

IN a small mixing bowl, combine the soy sauce, sugar, mushroom seasoning powder, and ¼ cup water and stir well. Set it near the stove.

HEAT the oil in a large nonstick skillet over medium-high heat until it shimmers. Add the rice cakes and cook, stirring occasionally, until the edges turn golden, about 1 minute. Add the garlic and cook, stirring, until fragrant but not colored, 15 to 30 seconds.

ADD the mushroom seasoning powder mixture and stir-fry occasionally until the liquid reduces to a glaze and the rice cakes have softened to the texture of chewy al dente pasta, about 2 minutes. Stir in the inari, serve on plates, and garnish with nothing.

SPICY STICKY RICE CAKES

SERVES 4 TO 6

On my first trip to Korea, tteok-bokki was my most-stopped-for dish. I'd trek across Seoul to try a famous version. I'd detour after spotting a vendor hovering over a particularly promising tray of these cylindrical rice cakes swimming in fire-red sauce, even if I was on the way home from dinner. Visually, at least, they reminded me of the cocktail wieners in BBQ sauce I'd see in my grandma's Crock-Pot back in Oklahoma—more so when I occasionally saw actual hot dogs in there with the rice cakes. The texture and flavor, though, were totally different, of course, the rice cakes slick and chewy, the sauce sweet and spicy.

When I make it at home, I use inari instead of fish cakes, because I love the way the chewy squares of marinated fried tofu sponge up the sauce, and add a little yellow pickled radish (takuan if you're shopping in a Japanese market or danmuji if you're in a Korean one) for crunch and brightness. You can skip the sil-gochu garnish, but the delicate slivers of dried chili look super-cool and add great flavor without heat.

4 scallions, trimmed

½ cup thinly sliced fresh pretty spicy red chilies, like Fresnos

½ cup maple syrup or agave syrup

2 tablespoons granulated sugar

2 tablespoons gochujang (Korean red chili paste)

1½ tablespoons gochugaru (Korean chili flakes)

1 tablespoon Mushroom Seasoning Powder, homemade (page 231) or store-bought

1 tablespoon soy sauce

1 teaspoon finely chopped garlic

1 pound Korean rice cake sticks, thawed if frozen, soaked in cold water for 30 minutes and drained well

2 cups drained inari (about 20)

1 cup half-moon slices (¼ inch) yellow pickled radish

4 generous pinches sil-gochu (Korean chili threads)

No-Cook Hot Sauce (page 229)

MAKE THE SAUCE:

PUT the scallions on a work surface and use the flat of a chef's knife blade to firmly whack the whites to smash them. Cut the scallions into 1-inch pieces.

PUT the scallions in a large high-sided skillet along with the chilies, maple syrup, sugar, gochujang, gochugaru, mushroom seasoning powder, soy sauce, garlic, and 2 cups water. Bring to a boil over high heat, stirring frequently, and cook until the sugar has fully dissolved, about 45 seconds.

MAKE THE DISH:

STIR in the rice cakes and inari, cover, and adjust the heat to cook at a moderate simmer, stirring occasionally, until the rice cakes are fully tender but chewy and the sauce clings to the rice cakes but is still saucy, about 4 minutes.

SERVE on plates with the pickled radish, sil-gochu, and some hot sauce.

CRISPY RICE CAKES WITH GARLIC SOY AND PUMPKIN

SERVES 4 TO 6

The long cylindrical rice cakes called garaetteok are so good simmered in sauce for tteok-bokki (page 190). When you roast them—or deep-fry them, as we do at the restaurant—they develop a crackly, crisp exterior. They remind me of perfectly roasted potatoes, actually, except instead of a soft, creamy interior, it's a soft, chewy-gooey one.

From there, you can go in so many directions. Here's one I often make at home, quick and easy with a garlicky sweet-salty glaze and chunks of roasted kabocha. Serve it with kimchi or perilla leaves.

4 cups (24 ounces) Korean rice cake sticks, soaked in cold water for 30 minutes and drained well

4 cups peeled, sliced (3 inches by ¾ inch) kabocha

¼ cup plus 2 tablespoons extra-virgin olive oil

1 teaspoon kosher salt

5 garlic cloves, thinly sliced

1 cup Korean rice syrup, corn syrup, or maple syrup

¼ cup soy sauce

2 tablespoons granulated sugar

1 tablespoon aonori

½ teaspoon coarsely ground black pepper

PREHEAT the oven to 375°F.

COMBINE the rice cakes, kabocha, ¼ cup of the oil, and the salt in a medium mixing bowl, stir to coat well, and transfer to one or two large sheet pans in a single layer.

ROAST, rotating and switching the positions of the sheet pan halfway through, until the kabocha is tender and lightly browned and the rice cakes are crisp on the outside and soft and chewy inside, about 15 minutes.

WHILE they roast, put the garlic and the remaining 2 tablespoons oil in a large wok, Dutch oven, or other wide high-sided pan, set it over high heat, and let the oil sizzle. Cook until the garlic is light golden, about 1 minute. Add the rice syrup, soy sauce, sugar, and ½ cup water and bring to a boil. Cook, stirring frequently, for 30 seconds. Take it off the heat and cover to keep warm.

WHEN the rice cakes and pumpkin are done, transfer them to the wok. Turn the heat back to high, toss to coat well, and cook, stirring constantly, until the sauce thickens to glaze the rice cakes and kabocha, about 1 minute. The kabocha will break up a little, and that's just fine. Serve right away in bowls, sprinkled with the aonori and pepper.

SWEET STICKY RICE LOTUS LEAF PARCELS

MAKES 16

I can't do dim sum without ordering lo mai gai. It's a thrill to open the lotus leaf packages to reveal steamy sticky rice studded with all sorts of savory treats. Once at Congee Village, in Flushing, Queens, I thought I was asking for lo mai gai, but I actually got zongzi, which is also sticky rice but gift-wrapped in bamboo leaf and studded with other savory treats. I later learned zongzi comes in sweet versions, too, with adzuki beans or jujubes. All of which probably set me off on this particular culinary detour.

The syrupy soy sauce mixture that coats the sticky rice here approaches dessert-level sweetness. The dates and chestnuts take it even closer. But then the earthy flavor of the lotus leaf wrapper, charred on a blazing charcoal grill (or with a torch or under the broiler), keeps it right on the edge. It's confusingly delicious.

Note: If you can't find lotus leaves at your local market or online, thawed frozen banana leaves are another great option here, though they'll impart a different flavor. The dish is well worth the bit of advance prep it requires. Plus, you can do the soak and wrapping, then keep these around in the fridge for a few days or in the freezer for a few months.

FOR THE PREP

4 cups short-grain sweet (glutinous) rice

1 cup dried black soybeans

2 tablespoons forbidden black rice

FOR THE DISH

4 dried lotus leaves

¾ cup granulated sugar

½ cup soy sauce

2 cups (12 ounces) quartered roasted chestnuts

1 cup pitted, quartered dates

2-inch knob ginger, peeled and finely chopped

SOAK THE RICE AND SOYBEANS:

IN a large mixing bowl, combine the sweet rice, soybeans, and forbidden rice and cover with several inches of water. Let soak for at least 4 hours or up to 6 hours.

FORM THE PARCELS:

ONCE the mixture has soaked, drain it, then rinse it under running water and drain well. Transfer the mixture to an electric rice cooker along with 2½ cups water. Cover, press the button, and let it cook. Meanwhile, cut off the thick nub from each lotus leaf, then quarter the leaves. Put them in a medium mixing bowl, cover with warm water, and let soak for 30 minutes. Drain them and pat dry.

PUT the sugar in a medium-heavy skillet over medium-low heat. Cook, stirring constantly, until it starts to clump, then melt, then turn an amber color, 6 to 8 minutes. While stirring, gradually pour in ¼ cup warm water (hot steam, stand back!) and keep stirring until any sugar crystals melt. Add the soy sauce and gently simmer over low heat, stirring occasionally, until it barely coats a spoon, about 10 minutes. Let it cool.

WHEN the rice is cooked, dump it into a large mixing bowl. Add the chestnuts, dates, and ginger and stir gently but well, then drizzle in the soy glaze and fold it in so the rice grains are all coated.

TO make the packets, work with one piece of lotus leaf at a time. Spoon about ½ cup of the rice mixture onto the center and flatten it a little. Fold the bottom edge of the lotus leaf over the rice, then fold in the sides, then roll it toward the top edge to make a package. To secure them, use toothpicks or cut long thin strips from one of the remaining lotus leaves and use them to tie the package. Repeat with the remaining leaves and rice. Wrapped, they keep in the fridge for up to 4 days.

FINISH THE DISH:

IF they're cold, warm them through in a 350°F oven or on an area of medium heat on the grill.

USE a clean kitchen towel to rub a thin layer of oil on the parcels. Char them on a hot area of the grill or under the broiler until the lotus leaf is blackened on both sides, 2 to 3 minutes per side. Serve hot.

SPICY CRISPY RICE SALAD

SERVES 4 TO 6

Kris Yenbamroong, of Night + Market in LA, blew my mind with his yam naem khao thawt, a Thai dish of crispy rice tossed with lots of tasty stuff from herbs and peanuts to ginger and pork sausage to, most memorably for me, a brutal amount of chilies, both dried and fresh. The result is incredible, so many different textures joined by a sweet-salty-tart dressing and electrified, thanks to all those chilies, by the same pain-and-pleasure principle we often operated on at Mission.

His version is untouchable, but ever since I watched him make it, I've been making my own. Besides veganizing the ingredients, I also cheat a little and buy puffed rice from a Thai market or, if I can't make it there, fry up purchased parboiled rice. You can adjust the heat level, though one of my favorite parts about the dish is how it hurts but keeps you coming back for more.

FOR THE CRISPY RICE

Neutral oil for deep-frying
(about 2 quarts)

1½ cups uncooked parboiled rice

FOR THE SALAD

¼ cup agave syrup

¼ cup lime juice (about 5 juicy limes)

¼ cup Thai seasoning sauce, such as
Golden Mountain

¾ teaspoon toasted sesame oil

¾ cup salted roasted peanuts

Handful mint leaves

¼ cup finely chopped fresh red
Thai bird chilies (about 20)

3-inch knob ginger, peeled and finely
chopped

1½ tablespoons store-bought dried
Thai chili powder

2 heaping teaspoons store-bought
Thai rice powder

FRY THE RICE:

HEAT 2 inches of neutral oil to 350°F (use a candy or deep-fry thermometer) in a medium pot over medium-high heat. Line a sheet pan with paper towels.

WHEN the oil is hot enough, fry the rice in three batches. Add the first batch and fry until the rice puffs and turns golden brown, 15 to 30 seconds per batch. Use a fine-mesh strainer to transfer each batch to the paper towels and spread them out a bit. Let the rice sit on the paper towels for at least 15 minutes to drain excess oil.

MAKE THE SALAD:

COMBINE the agave, lime juice, seasoning sauce, and sesame oil in a small mixing bowl and stir well.

COMBINE the puffed rice, peanuts, mint, fresh chilies, ginger, chili powder, and half the rice powder in a large mixing bowl and mix well. Just before you serve, add the lime mixture, mix well, and serve in bowls sprinkled with the remaining rice powder.

SWEET TREATS

SANDY'S PURPLE SWEET POTATOES

There are few things I like more than finding out what my friends love to eat and serving it to them with my own twist. For example, my friend Sandy Liang, whose family owns and operates the excellent Congee Village restaurants in New York, is obsessed with the Okinawan purple sweet potato. So I worked up this dish to elevate its pleasingly dry flesh and mellow honeyed sweetness. Steaming the potato keeps the sweetness subtle and the dessert clean and (relatively) light. Drizzling on condensed coconut milk—you can make it or buy it!—to keep things dairy free. Peanuts add crunch and some luscious Luxardo cherries and their syrup complete the picture.

FOR THE CONDENSED COCONUT MILK

1½ cups well-shaken unsweetened coconut milk

½ cup plus 1 tablespoon granulated sugar

FOR THE DESSERT

4 medium purple sweet potatoes, preferably Okinawan

8 Luxardo cherries, plus 2 tablespoons of their syrup

2 tablespoons roughly chopped salted roasted peanuts

MAKE THE CONDENSED COCONUT MILK:

COMBINE the coconut milk and sugar in a small saucepan and stir well. Bring to a vigorous simmer over high heat, then adjust the heat to cook at a steady simmer, stirring occasionally, until it turns a shade darker and reduces by about half, about 25 minutes. Let it cool slightly, then transfer to a container and refrigerate uncovered until chilled and thickened.

IT keeps in an airtight container in the fridge for up to 2 weeks.

MAKE THE DESSERT:

PREHEAT the oven to 350°F.

WRAP each potato in foil, put them on a sheet pan, and bake until very soft, about 1 hour.

UNWRAP the potatoes, cut a slit in the tops, and give the flesh a few presses with a fork. Put them on plates, drizzle about 1 tablespoon of the condensed coconut milk onto each one, then garnish with the cherries, peanuts, and cherry syrup.

BURNT BANANA WITH BLUEBERRIES AND WALNUTS

SERVES 4

I spend a lot of time at Hasaki, a sushi bar in the East Village. And every time, I get the banana dessert: the skin of the fruit blackened and flaking, the flesh warm and rich, almost custardy. It's so good I assumed that like a lot of Japanese food, making it required intricate technique or meticulous method. After years of going there, I finally asked how they did it, and the chef brought me to the kitchen, where he proceeded to use not a binchōtan-fired yakitori grill, but rather tongs and a beat-up stove's gas flame.

At Hasaki, the fire-roasted banana comes topped with green tea ice cream, which is obviously a winner. Here, I serve it with a mess of burst blueberries for a sweet-tart foil and raw walnuts for crunch and sugar-balancing bitterness.

FOR THE SAUCE

2 cups blueberries

½ cup granulated sugar

1 lemon

FOR THE DISH

4 ripe bananas, unpeeled

¼ cup roughly chopped raw walnuts

MAKE THE SAUCE:

COMBINE the blueberries and sugar in a medium saucepan. Stir in the finely grated zest and juice from half of the lemon. Save the rest for another purpose.

BRING the mixture to a boil over high heat, then reduce the heat to cook at a simmer until some blueberries burst and the sauce thickens to a slightly syrupy texture, about 10 minutes. Let it cool completely.

MAKE THE DISH:

RIGHT before you serve, set two stovetop burners to medium-high and roast the bananas directly over the flame, rotating and turning them over to cook them evenly, until the bananas are completely blackened all over, about 5 minutes. I like to use wire racks set over the flame, because it makes it easier to evenly blacken, though the racks will warp and discolor.

TO serve, use tongs (the bananas will be hot) to remove the peel alongside one side of each banana to reveal the flesh and put them flesh-side up on plates. Spoon on the blueberry sauce, sprinkle on the walnuts, and serve.

SEAWEED RICE KRISPIES TREATS

MAKES 16

During my stint at Blowfish Sushi in San Francisco, one of the cooks made us snacks on our break. Isa was born in Hawaii, and he modeled his impromptu concoctions on Hurricane Popcorn, created at a pushcart on Oahu. The story goes that the cart sold popcorn with all manner of mix-ins, and locals kept asking for nori and the soy sauce–seasoned rice crackers called arare. Isa's version had M&M's and aonori (a dried powdered seaweed the chefs had been using for some fanciful sushi roll), and I was so into the sweet-salty combo, the oldest dessert trick in the book. This is kind of like that, but in Rice Krispies Treats form.

Note: Strict vegans, make sure you use a vegan brand of crisp rice cereal, since some contain added vitamins derived from animals.

¼ cup plus 2 tablespoons unsalted vegan butter, plus a thin layer for the pan

½ teaspoon pure vanilla extract

8 ounces (about 2¼ cups) vegan mini marshmallows

5 cups vegan crispy rice cereal

1½ teaspoons toasted sesame seeds

1½ teaspoons aonori

¼ cup kizami (shredded) nori or thinly sliced nori

LINE a 9 x 13-inch baking/casserole dish with parchment paper and rub on a thin layer of vegan butter.

POUR an inch or so of water into a medium saucepan, bring it to a boil over medium-high heat, then reduce the heat to medium-low. Set a large heatproof mixing bowl in the saucepan, add the vegan butter and vanilla, and let the vegan butter melt completely. Fold in the marshmallows and cook, stirring occasionally, until the marshmallows lose their shape and become stretchy, 5 to 7 minutes. The butter won't fully mix with the marshmallows, and that's OK. Take the bowl off the heat and fold in the cereal to coat it as well as you can in the mixture.

POUR the mixture into the casserole dish and press into an even layer. Let it cool. Cut into 16 squares, transfer to a platter, and garnish with the sesame seeds, aonori, and kizami nori.

PEANUT BRITTLE

MAKES 2 QUARTS

When I was a kid, I ate peanut brittle because it was always around, and it was around because my dad was as fond of the snappy, nutty confection as I was of hiding out in my room listening to the Smashing Pumpkins. And even though I wasn't a dessert person, I was constantly snacking on the brittle from Russell Stover my dad kept in the minivan or raiding the pie table on holidays for the stuff my aunt brought.

Until I decided to make some for this book, I hadn't eaten peanut brittle for a solid two decades. But when I finally got this recipe down, the flavor totally took me back, and I remembered why I couldn't resist its charms.

3 cups granulated sugar

1⅛ cups light corn syrup

3 cups raw peanuts

1 tablespoon unsalted vegan butter

2½ tablespoons baking soda

1 teaspoon pure vanilla extract

LINE a large sheet pan with wax paper or a silicone mat.

IN a Dutch oven or medium pot that's nice and deep (since when you add the baking soda later, the mixture will bubble up), bring the sugar, corn syrup, and ½ cup water to a boil over high heat, stirring occasionally. Lower the heat and simmer until the syrup reaches the "thread stage," about 5 minutes. Unless you're familiar with the stages of sugar syrup, I recommend a candy thermometer here; it should read 230 to 235°F.

STIR in the peanuts and cook until the nuts turn tan and start to smell roasted and the candy thermometer registers 290°F, about 12 minutes. Remove from heat and stir in the vegan butter, baking soda, and vanilla. Watch it bubble! Stir really well to distribute the baking soda.

IMMEDIATELY pour the brittle onto the prepared baking sheet. Cool completely, about 30 minutes. Alternatively, while the brittle is still warm, sandwich it between silicone baking sheets or wax paper and roll out to a thin layer (about ¼ inch) with a rolling pin. Once the brittle cools, break it into pieces.

THE peanut brittle keeps covered at room temperature for up to 1 week.

DIVINITY

MAKES ABOUT 20 SQUARES

I miss this candy, because it reminds me of church bake sales and rest-stop snacking in Oklahoma. And because it's really good. Divinity is nougat adjacent, traditionally made with egg whites but swapped out here to great effect by aquafaba—also known as the liquid found in cans of chickpeas. My mom would often add pecans from the tree in our backyard to her chewy squares, and when I make it, I add sweet, buttery pine nuts, too.

A little neutral oil or nonstick spray

¼ cup liquid from a can of chickpeas (aka aquafaba)

2 cups granulated sugar

¼ cup light corn syrup

⅛ teaspoon kosher salt

1 teaspoon pure vanilla extract

¼ cup chopped pecans

¼ cup pine nuts

OIL a small sheet pan or spritz it with nonstick spray.

INTO the bowl of a stand mixer (or if you're using a handheld mixer, into a medium mixing bowl), pour the chickpea liquid and use the whisk attachment to whip on high speed until stiff peaks form, about 2 minutes.

IN a small heavy pot, bring the sugar, corn syrup, salt, and 1 cup water to a boil over high heat. Lower the heat and simmer over medium-high heat until the syrup reaches the "hard ball stage" (a candy thermometer should read 250 to 266°F), about 10 minutes. Turn off the heat.

WORK quickly now, so the sugar syrup doesn't cool. With the mixer on high speed again, add the vanilla to the bowl, then add the sugar syrup in a thin steady stream. Once it's all added, the mixture will look like nougat. Stop the mixer and fold in the pecans and pine nuts with a flexible spatula until well distributed.

POUR the mixture onto the prepared sheet pan and spread to an even ½-inch-thick layer (it might not cover the entire pan). Let it cool completely. Cut it like brownies into 2-inch squares.

IT keeps covered at room temperature for up to 1 week. If you need to stack them, separate them with wax paper so they don't stick together.

MICROWAVE MOCHI WITH SESAME GANACHE

MAKES 14

One day, Mino wanted mochi, and I thought, OK, let's make it. But a YouTube search killed our fun. Because we were watching people whack steamed glutinous rice (a short-grain variety called mochigome) with giant wooden mallets in order to produce an edible dough with that amazing texture—silky and soft, springy and stretchy.

We kept searching, though, and came across really cool microwave methods that lean on mochiko, labeled "sweet rice flour" but basically just cooked mochigome that's dried and ground. After that, we tinkered a bit, and what do you know? We had pretty damn good mochi that I filled with a nuke-then-freeze ganache made with white chocolate, tahini, and coconut milk. Try it and you'll see that just as there's nothing like fresh Krispy Kreme, there's nothing like fresh mochi. Even this mochi.

Note: Many white chocolates contain milk solids, so strict vegans should make sure to use vegan brands.

FOR THE FILLING

7 ounces vegan white chocolate, chopped into chip-size pieces

1 tablespoon well-stirred tahini (I love Soom)

⅓ cup plus 1 tablespoon coconut milk

Neutral oil for greasing the pan

FOR THE MOCHI

1½ cups mochiko sweet rice flour

3 tablespoons granulated sugar

½ cup cornstarch, plus more for dusting

Powdered sugar, for dusting

2 teaspoons toasted black sesame seeds

MAKE THE FILLING:

COMBINE the chocolate and tahini in a medium heatproof mixing bowl and stir well. In a medium microwave-safe bowl, microwave the coconut milk on high in 30-second intervals until it bubbles gently, stopping before it boils, about 1 minute total. Pour the coconut milk into the mixing bowl and stir until the chocolate has fully melted and the mixture is smooth.

LIGHTLY grease a small sheet pan, then pour the mixture onto the pan. Freeze, uncovered, until solid but still malleable, about 1 hour. Scoop out 1 tablespoon's worth, roll it into a ball, and put it on a plate. Do the same with the rest, then put them back on the sheet pan and put it back in the freezer while you make the mochi.

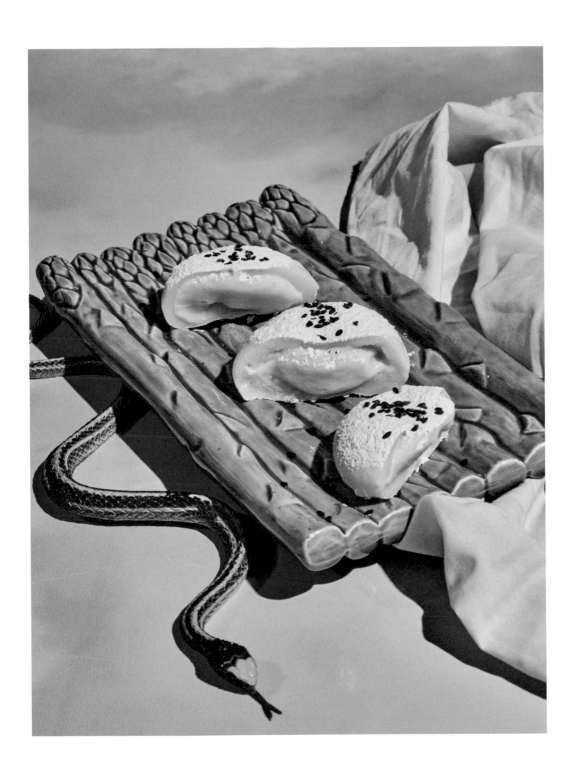

MAKE THE MOCHI:

COMBINE the mochiko, sugar, and 1½ cups water in a medium microwave-safe bowl and stir until smooth. Cover with plastic wrap and microwave on high for 1½ minutes. Uncover, scrape down the sides of the bowl with a flexible spatula, stir well, and microwave on high again until it looks glossy and translucent, about 30 seconds more.

UNCOVER and stir in a single direction (say, clockwise) until it cools and thickens to form what looks like dough, about 1 minute. This helps give it its chewy texture.

DUST a clean work surface with cornstarch and add ½ cup or so of cornstarch to a small mixing bowl. To make each mochi, dip a spoon in cornstarch, spoon out a scant ¼ cup of the mochiko mixture, put it on the dusted surface, and flatten it to an approximately 3-inch circle. Repeat for the rest of the mochiko mixture. Add one of the frozen ganache balls, gather the edges of the mochi around the ball to fully enclose it, and pinch them together, twisting off the pinched part. Place them pinched-side down on a plate and repeat for the rest of the mochiko mixture and ganache.

THEY'RE ready to eat. Or you can freeze them in an airtight container in the freezer for up to 1 month. Let them thaw for 10 minutes to eat them like mochi ice cream or thaw fully.

TO serve, add a little powdered sugar to a mesh strainer and tap it against your palm to dust over each mochi. Sprinkle on the black sesame seeds.

JIM'S GERMAN CHOCOLATE CAKE

MAKES ONE 9-INCH TWO-LAYER CAKE

Every year, my mom made this for my dad's birthday, a rich chocolate cake with coconut-pecan icing that's as German as I am. (The story goes that a Texan sent in a recipe to a local newspaper for a cake she made using a kind of baking chocolate created by a guy named Samuel German.)

Unlike my mom, I'm not a good baker, but I'm proud to say I actually figured out this butter- and egg-free recipe myself, Frankensteining about a hundred recipes from the Internet until I made something that takes me right back to hers. Making it both vegan and delicious wasn't hard—as any fan of boxed cake mix knows, oil (plus some applesauce and oat milk) makes a moist cake.

FOR THE CAKE

½ cup canola oil, plus more for the pans

2 cups all-purpose flour, plus more for the pans

¾ cup natural unsweetened cocoa powder

2 teaspoons baking powder

1½ teaspoons baking soda

1¾ cups granulated sugar

1 teaspoon kosher salt

1 cup unsweetened oat milk

⅔ cup unsweetened applesauce

1 tablespoon apple cider vinegar

1 tablespoon pure vanilla extract

FOR THE ICING

Two 13.5-ounce cans well-shaken unsweetened coconut milk (3½ cups)

1¼ cups plus 1 tablespoon granulated sugar

1¼ cups (7 ounces) chopped pecans

1 cup sweetened coconut flakes

1 teaspoon pure vanilla extract

¼ teaspoon kosher salt

MAKE THE CAKE:

PREHEAT the oven to 350°F. Line two 9-inch round or square baking pans with parchment paper, then oil and flour them.

SIFT the flour, cocoa, baking powder, and baking soda into a large mixing bowl or bowl of a stand mixer. Add the sugar and salt and use a handheld mixer or stand mixer to whisk on low speed to combine. Add the oat milk, applesauce, oil, vinegar, and vanilla. Whisk on high speed until well combined and smooth.

BRING 1 cup water to a boil. Reduce the speed to low and in a thin, steady stream, pour in the water. Increase the speed to high and whisk for 30 seconds to incorporate some air. Divide the batter between the two prepared pans. Bake on the center rack until a toothpick inserted in the center of the cake comes out clean, about 30 minutes. Let the cakes cool in the pans for 10 minutes. Remove from the pans and cool completely on a rack before frosting.

MAKE THE ICING:

COMBINE the coconut milk and sugar in a medium skillet and stir well. Bring to a vigorous simmer over high heat, then adjust the heat to cook at a steady simmer, stirring occasionally, until it turns a shade darker and reduces by about half, 25 to 35 minutes. Let it cool slightly, then stir in the pecans, coconut flakes, vanilla, and salt. Transfer to a container and refrigerate uncovered until chilled and thickened, at least 2 hours.

FROST THE CAKE:

SCOOP 1 cup of the frosting onto one of the cake layers and spread to coat the top evenly. Top with the other cake layer and do the same with another 1 cup of the frosting. Use an offset spatula to evenly cover the sides.

STORE the cake in an airtight container for up to 3 days.

SAUCES AND SEASONINGS

LEMON KOSHO

There are four ingredients in this sauce, though no one who tries it will believe you. The flavor is so incredibly complex—salty and floral, a bright-but-subdued acidity, the exhilarating bitterness of the peel and pith. It reminds me of a lemon version of yuzu kosho, the Japanese condiment made with yuzu zest, and preserved lemons, the North African pickle that we used to blend to make it. When one day we ran out of preserved lemons, I grabbed a few fresh from the bartender to throw together a desperate stand-in sauce. I was so happy with the result that I couldn't believe I didn't do it in the first place.

Turns out it's also a great way to, well, preserve lemons, since the creamy puree lasts for a couple weeks in the fridge.

Try it with fragrant fried rice (see gage 172), plain rice, or with roasted vegetables.

2 lemons, stem nubs trimmed

2 tablespoons chopped oil-cured Calabrian chilies (about 6) or fresh red Thai chilies

2 tablespoons kosher salt

⅔ cup extra-virgin olive oil

QUARTER the lemons, flick out the seeds, then chop, skin and all, into ¼-inch pieces. Put them in a blender, add the chilies and salt, and blend on low speed to a thick puree, about 45 seconds. Scrape down the sides of the blender, then add the oil and ½ cup water and blend on high speed until it's as smooth as possible, about 1 minute.

IT keeps in an airtight container in the fridge for up to 2 weeks.

WHIPPED GARLIC SAUCE

MAKES ABOUT 2 CUPS

I know the boldly garlicky, fluffy emulsion from Lebanese called toum, not from travels to Tripoli but from trips to the cold section at Sahadi's, an incredible Lebanese-run grocery store in Brooklyn. Toum is magic for vegans, because it delivers that luscious creamy aioli texture without eggs. I add mustard, because I like the little bite it brings and because for the home cook, it provides a little insurance against the sauce breaking while it's in the processor. On the off chance it does, a teaspoon or so of ice water fixes it right up.

Try it slicked on roasted or grilled vegetables or on the side of Mung Bean Pancakes (page 63).

½ cup peeled garlic cloves (about 30)

1 teaspoon kosher salt

1 teaspoon Dijon mustard

1 juicy lemon

1¾ cups extra-virgin olive oil

PUT the garlic and salt in a food processor and process until the garlic is minced. Scrape down the sides of the processor bowl with a spatula, then add the mustard and the finely grated zest and juice of the lemon. Pulse to combine.

WITH the machine running, add the oil in a slow, thin stream, and once you've added all of the oil, keep processing just until the mixture is creamy, thick, and fluffy, like mayonnaise. If it goes from thick to runny, gradually add ice water (a teaspoon at a time) and process until it's thick and creamy again.

TRANSFER the garlic cream to an airtight container and keep in the fridge for up to 1 week.

TART GARLIC SAUCE

MAKES ABOUT 2¾ CUPS

This creamy, tangy puree is inspired by a Greek garlic sauce I love but also reminds me, with the slow-fried garlic and pepperoncini (reminiscent of a pickled chili popular in Chengdu), of the base of a certain Sichuan stew. It's makes a great dip for raw vegetables or dressing for grilled ones. Or try it on roasted eggplant (see page 80), roasted squash (see page 77), or smashed cucumbers (see page 49), either instead of, or in addition to, the tingly granola.

2 cups peeled garlic cloves

1 cup extra-virgin olive oil

1 generous cup finely chopped drained, stemmed pepperoncini

½ cup red wine vinegar

1 tablespoon drained capers

1 tablespoon Dijon mustard

PREHEAT the oven to 250 F.

IN a small ovenproof saucepan (it should be narrow enough for 1 cup of oil to submerge the garlic), combine the garlic cloves and olive oil and bring to a gentle bubble over medium heat. Cover the pan, transfer it to the oven, and cook until the garlic is smooshably soft, 20 to 25 minutes. Let it cool completely.

TRANSFER the mixture to a blender, add the pepperoncini, vinegar, capers, and mustard, and blend on high until completely smooth and creamy. Refrigerate to chill before serving. It gets a little thicker and that's good.

IT keeps in the fridge for up to 2 weeks.

CHARRED CHILI PASTE (RED AND GREEN)

MAKES ABOUT 2 CUPS

For me this coarse puree brings back some of my best Oklahoma food memories, in particular the salsa especial at Chelino's made with roasted tomatoes and charred jalapeños and Jimbo's green chili cheeseburgers, a New Mexico–born triumph fueled by the beauty of Hatch chilies and one that I'd squirt with yellow mustard and demolish.

The condiment here channels the combo of tartness and that grassy, bitter-edged fire-roasted chili flavor, which we mimic using a mix of poblanos and serranos. It's so good that practically every time we were workshopping a dish, we'd say, "Well, this dish would be even better with some acid, heat, and umami . . . let's add the chili paste!"

Our supplier messed up one day and sent ripe jalapeños, and we realized red chilies were great here, too, with a slightly fruitier flavor profile.

RED VERSION

¼ cup unseasoned rice vinegar

1 tablespoon Mushroom Seasoning Powder, homemade (page 231) or store-bought

1 pound moderately spicy fresh red chilies, such as Korean, Fresno, or ripe jalapeño (about 30)

2 tablespoons extra-virgin olive oil

GREEN VERSION

¼ cup unseasoned rice vinegar

1 tablespoon Mushroom Seasoning Powder, homemade (page 231) or store-bought

1 pound poblano chilies (about 5)

½ pound serrano or small jalapeño chilies (about 15)

2 tablespoons extra-virgin olive oil

STIR together the vinegar and mushroom seasoning powder in a small mixing bowl.

POSITION an oven rack about 4 inches from the broiler and preheat the broiler. Put the chilies on a sheet pan, drizzle with the oil, and toss well to coat them. Arrange them in a single layer and broil, turning over the chilies once about halfway through, until they're blistered and blackened, 8 to 10 minutes for the red chilies and about 20 minutes for the green chilies. Let them cool a bit.

PULL the stems off the chilies, but don't deseed them or remove the skins. Add the chilies to a food processor and pulse until fairly finely chopped, then add the vinegar mixture and pulse until well mixed but still a little chunky.

IT keeps in the fridge for up to 1 month.

GRAPEFRUIT GOCHUJANG

MAKES ABOUT 2 CUPS

Segments of grapefruit, supremed so they're free of membrane and a pleasure to chomp on, add a new dimension of flavor to the sweet, spicy sauce you typically eat with bibimbap (page 180). So does the grapefruit's zest, which is fragrant and bitter in a good way. The bitterness is so welcome here that you don't have to fear the white pith when zesting. I also recommend, if you've got one, a grater with slightly larger holes than ones you typically use for zesting.

Besides bibimbap, try it on crispy fried foods and as a dressing for salads once you crush the grapefruit segments a bit, so it's nice and runny.

½ cup gochujang (Korean red chili paste)

½ cup Korean rice syrup, maple syrup, or agave syrup

¼ cup unseasoned rice or white vinegar

2 tablespoons soy sauce

1 tablespoon finely chopped garlic

1 teaspoon Mushroom Seasoning Powder, homemade (page 231) or store-bought

3 large red grapefruits

IN a small mixing bowl, whisk together the gochujang, rice syrup, vinegar, soy sauce, garlic, and mushroom seasoning powder until smooth. It keeps in an airtight container in the fridge for a few months.

UP to a day or so before you serve it, finely grate the grapefruit zest into the gochujang mixture. Next, cut off each end of the grapefruits to reveal the flesh, then stand them up and carve off the peel and pith. Working over a bowl, cut the segments away from the membrane, letting any juice drip into the bowl. When you're done, squeeze the juice from the remaining membrane into the bowl.

ADD the grapefruit segments and juice to the mixture and fold to combine.

SCALLION-MISO DIP

MAKES ABOUT 1 CUP

I don't think I've ever been to EN Japanese Brasserie, in the West Village, and not ordered the onion-miso dip. Served with raw asparagus, greens-on radishes, and slender young carrots in warmer months and steamed mountain yam, lotus root, and kabocha in colder ones, it has this really intense savory sort of sweetness and a similar hit of umami to my other favorite onion dip (French, from the Lipton packet).

I like to eat it with super-cold crunchy raw vegetables, so give them a few minutes in ice water or, for a more dramatic presentation, pile on some crushed ice. Grilled and steamed vegetables—scallions, sweet potatoes, baby turnips—are awesome, too, as long as you hold back on any seasoning. The dip provides all the seasoning you'll need.

¼ cup red (aka) miso

2 tablespoons mirin

2 tablespoons dry sake

1 teaspoon gochugaru (Korean chili flakes)

2 cups thinly sliced scallions (about 10)

1 teaspoon finely chopped garlic

1 tablespoon neutral oil

1 tablespoon toasted sesame oil

2 tablespoons granulated sugar

IN a small mixing bowl, combine the miso, mirin, sake, and gochugaru and set aside.

COMBINE the scallions, garlic, and both oils in a medium-heavy skillet, set it over high heat, and let it start to sizzle. Cook, stirring and reducing the heat if necessary, until the scallions have softened but not browned, about 2 minutes. Add the mirin mixture and the sugar and cook, stirring, for 10 seconds. Turn off the heat and let it cool fully.

IT keeps in the fridge for up to 1 month.

GINGER-SCALLION SAUCE

MAKES ABOUT 3 CUPS

Few things on earth don't benefit from a spoonful of this sauce. Cooking super-briefly brings out the fragrance of scallions and ginger without totally taming their bite, so this bold, oily southern Chinese condiment brings a thrill to whatever it touches.

8 scallions, trimmed and very roughly chopped

¼ pound unpeeled ginger, washed well and roughly chopped

1½ cups olive or canola oil

1 tablespoon Mushroom Seasoning Powder, homemade (page 231) or store-bought

Scant 1 teaspoon granulated sugar

PULSE the scallions in a food processor just until finely chopped. Scrape into a large heatproof mixing bowl (large, because when you add hot oil it'll bubble up). Pulse the ginger in the food processor just until finely chopped, and add it to the bowl, too. Stir well.

HEAT the oil in a medium skillet over medium-high heat until it's very hot but not quite smoking, then pour it over the scallion-ginger mixture. Let it cool for a couple minutes, then stir in the mushroom seasoning powder and sugar and let it cool completely.

IT keeps in the fridge for up to 1 month. Stir well before using.

BLACK BEAN SAUCE

MAKES ABOUT 1½ CUPS

I was taught to make this Chinese-style sauce by stir-frying fermented black soybeans with ginger-scallion sauce. But I liked it so much, I started making a sort of all-in-one version, adding the black beans to the raw ginger and scallion before I poured on the scalding oil. A little sugar softens the amazing pungent, salty pop they contribute and chili adds a little zing.

Like tomato paste or bouillon cube, this sauce is used sparingly and along with flavorful liquids to deliver umami saltiness and complexity to anything from stir-fried vegetables to boiled noodles to steamed rice.

5 scallions, trimmed and very roughly chopped

2 ounces unpeeled ginger (a 3-inch knob), scrubbed and roughly chopped

½ cup Chinese fermented black beans, rinsed and roughly chopped

1 teaspoon finely chopped serrano or jalapeño chili

¼ teaspoon kosher salt

¾ cup extra-virgin olive oil

1 teaspoon Mushroom Seasoning Powder, homemade (page 231) or store-bought

¼ teaspoon granulated sugar

PULSE the scallions in a food processor just until finely chopped, then scrape them into a medium heatproof mixing bowl (not small, because when you add hot oil it'll bubble up). Pulse the ginger just until finely chopped, and add it to the bowl, too. Add the black beans, chili, and salt and stir well.

HEAT the oil in a medium skillet over medium-high heat until it's very hot but not quite smoking, then pour it over the black bean mixture. Let it hang out for a couple minutes, then stir in the mushroom seasoning powder and sugar. Let it cool completely.

IT keeps in the fridge for up to 1 month.

SMOKY COCONUT

MAKES ABOUT 3 CUPS

This preparation of coconut delivers some of the smoky, salty-sweet qualities that make bacon so beloved by meat eaters. At the restaurant, it requires a dehydrator and a smoker, but this quick version is just as tasty and all you need is your oven.

3 cups unsweetened shredded coconut

¼ cup maple syrup

1 tablespoon plus 1 teaspoon sweet smoked paprika

2 teaspoons kosher salt

PREHEAT the oven to 325°F.

MIX the ingredients well in a medium mixing bowl, spread in a single layer on a large baking sheet, and cook until the coconut turns golden, 6 to 8 minutes. Keep a close eye on it at the end of the cooking time, since coconut can go from white to golden pretty quickly.

LET it cool completely in the pan. It keeps in an airtight container in a cool, dark place for up to 1 month.

CASHEW CREAM

MAKES 2 CUPS

A big challenge of vegan cooking is figuring out how to add creamy textures and rich, fatty flavors without relying on dairy. One answer? Cashew cream—raw nuts soaked overnight then blended to a Hollandaise-like silkiness. I use it to finish stuffed roasted kabocha (page 77) and to make sure egg lovers don't miss the yolk that often tops bibimbap (page 180).

½ pound (1½ cups) raw cashews

1 teaspoon kosher salt

COMBINE the cashews with 3 cups water in a tall, narrow container (it's fine if they float) and let them soak in the fridge for at least 8 hours or overnight.

AFTER they've soaked, drain the cashews and put them in the blender with the salt and 1 cup fresh water. Blend on high speed until very smooth, 1 to 2 minutes.

IT keeps in an airtight container in the fridge for up to 1 week.

CHILI OIL

MAKES 1 QUART

Made in the classic Sichuan style, this chili oil is loosely based on the one I watched the legendary chef Yu Bo make in Chengdu. It's infused with medicinal spices like star anise and cardamom but made with gochugaru, the Korean chili flakes that I find are the closest approximation of the dried chilies he used, plus cayenne for color and extra heat.

It's great for finishing roasted eggplant (see page 80) and Chilled Tofu in Peanut Milk (page 119), Mapo Tofu (page 90), and Cumin-Flavor Tofu Skin (page 150). If you must, high-quality store-bought chili oil works OK, too.

1 cup (3½ ounces) gochugaru (Korean chili flakes)

2 tablespoons cayenne pepper

10 whole cloves

8 green cardamom pods, bruised

3 whole star anise

4 cups neutral oil, such as grapeseed

COMBINE the gochugaru, cayenne, cloves, cardamom, and star anise in a large heatproof mixing bowl and mix well.

IN a medium pot, heat the oil over high heat, stirring occasionally, until it registers 275°F on a thermometer. Immediately pour it over the spice mixture and let it all sit until completely cool, about 1 hour. Strain through a fine-mesh sieve, discarding the solids. It's fine if there's still some sediment in the oil.

IT keeps in the fridge for up to 3 months.

NO-COOK HOT SAUCE

MAKES 2 CUPS

I can't quite convince myself to make my own hot sauce, blooming aromatics and fermenting chilies, when there are so many good ones out there. And I'm not even talking about the artisanal ones. Give me a bottle of Crystal or Frank's RedHot and a few takeout egg rolls, and I'm happy. Still, I think it's very cool that you can take a jar of sambal oelek— an Indonesian sauce—and whiz it up with some vinegar to make a bright, silky sauce with great chili-forward flavor.

1 cup sambal oelek

1 cup distilled white vinegar

BLEND the sambal on high speed until you don't see any more seeds, about 1 minute, then add the vinegar and blend until smooth, about 30 seconds more.

IT keeps in an airtight container in the fridge for up to 3 months.

MUSHROOM STOCK

When I wanted to make a stock to give some of the soups and stews in this book a flavor-packed foundation, I thought about Turtle Tower, a northern Vietnamese restaurant in San Francisco where I spent many mornings hunched over a bowl of pho. The broth is so good I used it as inspiration for this one. Briefly charred scallions and onions contribute natural sweetness to balance the super-savory umami from mushrooms.

12 scallions, trimmed

¼ cup grapeseed or another neutral oil

2 cups sliced (½ inch) white onion

1-inch knob ginger, sliced

8 ounces dried shiitake

2 tablespoons Mushroom Seasoning Powder, homemade (page 231) or store-bought

PUT the scallions on a work surface and use the flat of a chef's knife blade to firmly whack the whites to smash them. Cut the scallions into 2-inch pieces.

HEAT 2 tablespoons of the oil in a large heavy pot or Dutch oven over high heat until it just begins to smoke. Add the scallions, stir to coat in the oil, and cook, stirring once or twice, until they begin to char at the edges, about 1 minute. Transfer the scallions to a plate, add the rest of the oil, and cook the onion the same way, 1 to 2 minutes. Return the scallions to the pot.

ADD 16 cups water, ginger, mushrooms, and mushroom seasoning powder, cover, and let it come to a boil, skimming off any froth. Reduce the heat and cook at a gentle simmer, partially covered, for 1½ hours, to extract the flavors. Strain, reserving the solids. When the mushrooms are cool enough to handle, squeeze them one by one into the stock to extract the liquid they've absorbed, then discard them and the remaining solids.

IT keeps in an airtight container in the fridge for up to 1 week or in the freezer for up to 3 months.

MUSHROOM SEASONING POWDER

MAKES 1 GENEROUS CUP

There are many sources of umami in this book, but this might be the one I look to most. Dried mushrooms team up with straight-up MSG to create a super-seasoning. Porcini give the mix a little more complexity and richness, but dried shiitake work well and cost less. Feel free to use a store-bought version, too, like Imperial Taste or Po Lo Ku brand mushroom seasoning.

1½ ounces dried porcini, dried shiitake, or a mixture (or ½ cup powdered)

½ cup MSG

¼ cup kosher salt

1 teaspoon granulated sugar

IF you're using whole mushrooms, work in batches to grind the dried mushrooms to a fine powder in a spice grinder. Sift each batch into a storage container. Add the MSG, salt, and sugar and mix really well.

IT keeps in the pantry for up to 1 month.

UMAMI SALT AND PEPPER

MAKES ABOUT 2 CUPS

This all-purpose seasoning delivers umami, salt, and multiple dimensions of peppercorn—the black adds sharpness, the white earthiness, and the pink (technically not a true peppercorn) a welcome fruity bite.

¾ cup homemade Mushroom Seasoning Powder (see above) or 1 cup (4 ounces) store-bought

⅓ cup black peppercorns

⅓ cup pink peppercorns

⅓ cup white peppercorns

MIX the ingredients in a bowl, then blend in batches in a spice grinder to a fine powder. Stir once more.

IT keeps in an airtight container in the pantry for up to 4 months, but begins to lose vibrancy after 2 weeks.

INGREDIENTS

TO RE-CREATE THE FLAVORS IN THIS BOOK AT HOME, you'll have to do some shopping. The good news is that finding Korean gochujang, Japanese inari, and Calabrian chilies is easier than ever, thanks to the internet. Still, I recommend visiting local markets because what you trade for convenience you make up for in the fun of roaming aisles full of products with which you might be unfamiliar. If you're like me, you can't help but buy a few things you didn't plan to buy, and you'll inevitably learn something new.

This list here includes common ingredients in this book that aren't necessarily self-explanatory, may have unclear labeling, or otherwise deserve some clarification.

AONORI

Aonori is a coarsely powdered seaweed used in Japanese cooking, most commonly in yakisoba, okonomiyaki, and takoyaki. It has a vivid green color and a bright, oceanic flavor. Buy it at Japanese grocery stores and online.

APPLE VINEGAR

One of my recipes calls for Japanese or Korean apple vinegar, and both have a nice subtle apple flavor that you don't find in apple cider vinegars. My favorite is the pricy-but-worth-it Japanese kind, which has a great sweet-and-sour quality, but the Korean ones work well for the purposes of this book, and if I'm honest, so does unseasoned rice vinegar.

CHILIES, FRESH

You'll see several varieties of fresh chilies in this book. Green serranos and jalapeños are both grassy and hot, with serranos on average providing a bit more of each, and available at Mexican markets and nowadays many chain supermarkets. Thai bird chilies, red and green, are smaller, narrower, and hotter and sold at many Asian markets and some big supermarkets as well as, of course, Thai markets. Long green chilies refer to any variety that's, well, long and green with moderate heat. Options for green include Anaheim, Cubanelle, Hatch, goat horn, and, ideally, the 4-ish-inch-long one sold at Korean markets. Options for moderately spicy red chilies include Fresno, ripe jalapeño, and the red chilies sold at Korean markets.

CHINKIANG VINEGAR

A few recipes call for this Chinese black vinegar made from glutinous rice. It's dark in color, fuller-bodied than many vinegars, and slightly malty with a bracing sourness. There's no substitute, but white rice vinegar mixed with a touch of soy sauce or tamari makes a decent stand-in.

CHRYSANTHEMUM GREENS

Finding these will probably require a trip to a Chinese, Korean, or Japanese market. Called *ssukgat* in Korean and *shungiku* in Japanese and occasionally labeled "crown daisy," the frilly leaves and thin stems are well worth seeking out for their super-green flavor. If you must, substitute another quick-cooking green like watercress.

DASIMA OR DASHI KOMBU

Known as *dasima* in Korean and *dashi kombu* in Japanese, this dried kelp packs tons of umami, which it imparts when steeped in water or broths. Look for dasima or dashi kombu in Asian markets, health food stores, and online.

DOENJANG

Sometimes labeled "soybean paste" and sold in jars and brown tubs at Korean markets, doenjang has some similarities to Japanese miso, but it's made with a different process and has a bolder flavor. I developed the recipes in this book with readily available brands of doenjang, though you can find finer long-fermented products out there, too.

DRIED BEAN CURD STICK

When fresh soy milk is simmered to make tofu, the skin that forms on the surface gets skimmed off and reserved, because it's a great ingredient on its own with a nice chew and ability to soak up sauces. Called *yuba* in Japanese, it's also dried in Chinese cooking and sold as these furrowed tan sticks. You can totally sub fresh yuba (Hodo Foods sells a good product), if you come across it. Otherwise, before use they should be soaked overnight and drained.

DRIED MIYEOK OR WAKAME

I use this blackish green seaweed in several recipes in this book for its awesome slick texture and subtle sea flavor. Called *miyeok* in Korean and *wakame* in Japanese, the dried versions are sold in small pieces or longer strips that you should snip with scissors into 1-inch pieces before measuring for these recipes. After it's rehydrated, a 1-ounce piece yields about 2 cups.

DRIED SHIITAKE

Not just a substitute for fresh, dried shiitakes offer a dense, chewy texture that holds up to long cooking and extra umami thanks to the drying process. Some people love the ones with really thick caps, but I like my dried shiitakes the way I like my chocolate chip cookies: nice and thin.

Dried shiitake are typically soaked before use in my recipes: Put them in a bowl, cover with hot water by an inch or so, and add a strainer or plate to keep the mushrooms submerged. Once they're soft, in 20 to 30 minutes, remove them, squeezing them gently to remove excess water. Discarding the soaking water, trim off any tough stems, and they're ready to go.

GOCHUGARU

Literally "chili flakes" in Korean, the product sold as gochugaru in Korean markets, some high-end grocery stores, and online is not the stuff you shake onto your pizza slices. Sun-dried before they're ground, these dried chilies bring a complex, bright (almost lemony) flavor. Many stores offer the chili flakes in three heat levels—mild, medium, or hot. I buy the medium when I can. Look for the coarsely ground product, not the finely ground one, for the recipes in this book. If you must, you can substitute generic red chili flakes.

GOCHUJANG

Sometimes labeled "hot pepper paste" and "red chili paste" and sold in jars and bright-red tubs at many markets nowadays, gochujang is a bold, spicy, umami-packed, slightly sweet ingredient made from fermented dried chilies. If it's sold in a squirt bottle, it's probably chogochujang, a sauce made *with* gochujang, which is a different product.

GOSARI (KOREAN FERN SHOOTS)

These are the young shoots or fiddleheads of an edible fern sometimes referred to as *fernbrake* or *bracken*. It's harvested, often wild, then boiled. I love the texture of the narrow shoots, which to me recalls that of cooked long beans—tender but chewy and a little squeaky. You can find them dried, but I like to buy the brownish boiled shoots sold in bags in the refrigerated case at Korean markets. If you can't find them, briefly blanched then julienned snow peas contribute a nice, if different, flavor and texture.

INARI

Also called *inari age*, this is tofu that's been deep-fried then simmered with soy sauce and sugar—it's chewy, sweet, and full of umami, and because I love it so, I add it to many dishes where its presence is not typical. It comes canned and vac-packed at Japanese grocery stores and online. Strict vegans should make sure the ingredient list doesn't include katsuobushi (a dried, cured fish used to make dashi).

INSTANT RAMYEON

When I was growing up, the main appeal of instant ramen (or ramyeon, as it's called in Korea) was its convenience (boil, mix, eat) and its price point. Since then, I've learned that, expediency aside, the product is beloved by many, especially in countries like Thailand and Korea, where it's just one of many delicious noodle options.

In this book, you'll spot the noodles and seasoning packets in a few recipes. Be sure to look for vegan brands, with seasoning packets that contain no animal derivatives. I really like the Korean Nongshim Soon brand.

KIMCHI

In this book you'll find several recipes for kimchi, from the fairly traditional (spicy cabbage, stuffed cucumber) to the modern (pineapple!). They all make tasty banchan, the little dishes that accompany a bigger meal. Spicy cabbage kimchi is the one you'll need for several recipes in this book, such as kimchi stew and army stew, and you can feel free to buy it or make it (see page 14). Keep in mind that kimchi from different makers will have slightly different flavor profiles, so find one you love and always season to taste. Also note that at least one recipe calls for a full quart of chopped cabbage kimchi and a cup of its brine, so when you're in the market, really stock up. If you're a strict vegan, be sure to look for kimchi made without fish sauce, salted shrimp, or oysters.

KOREAN RADISH OR DAIKON

For recipes in this book, you can use either of these radishes, both mild and crunchy when raw and sweet and juicy when cooked. Daikon is a bit easier to find in my experience. Their width varies, so when I call for half-moons, consider quarter-moons if they're very broad, so the pieces are bite-sized.

KOREAN RICE CAKES

I call for two shapes of the chewy tteok (Korean rice cakes) in these pages: cylindrical (sometimes labeled "sticks" or "for tteok-bokki") and sliced. Before using, soak them in cold water for 30 minutes, then drain them well. You'll find both at Korean markets, either in the refrigerated or frozen case.

KOREAN RICE SYRUP

Made from fermented rice, this sweet, slightly nutty brown syrup called ssal-jocheong gives sauces a beautiful glossiness thanks to its viscosity. Corn syrup is your best substitute, though its flavor is less complex. Maple or agave syrup make acceptable subs, too.

MIRIN

This is a relatively low-alcohol Japanese rice wine that's slightly sweet. Look for hon mirin, which is made from fermented rice. Many big brands sell what's known as aji mirin, a product made with added sweeteners, and that's just fine for my recipes. Dry sherry or Chinese Shaoxing wine work as substitutes.

MSG

There are many sources of monosodium glutamate in this cookbook, natural and not. Occasionally, I call for straight-up MSG in flaky crystal form, which is sold most commonly under the Ajinomoto brand. It adds pure umami, without any other flavor, and a touch of saltiness.

MUSHROOM SEASONING POWDER

This is one of my favorite ingredients for adding umami to vegan dishes. Labeled "Mushroom Seasoning," the coarse granules harness the power of dried mushrooms (and often MSG). Note that this isn't pure mushroom powder. It's a product that contains salt and sometimes sugar and the flavor varies slightly by brand. My homemade version (page 231) stays pretty true to the product I buy.

NEUTRAL OIL

When I call for neutral oil in this book, I mean oil without any notable flavor—for instance, grapeseed, vegetable, canola, or perhaps the healthiest and most expensive option, avocado oil. It's just the thing when you want to add or cook with fat but don't want the fruity, spicy vibes of olive oil or the toasty, nutty quality of sesame oil. It's also just right for higher heat cooking, since neutral-flavored oils tend to have higher smoke points.

NOODLES

Many of the noodles I call for in this book are Korean products. They're all readily available at Korean markets and online.

Naengmyeon are buckwheat noodles (just FYI, they're very much not the same as Japanese soba) often served chilled. They're super-chewy in a great way. Dangmyeon are sometimes labeled "sweet potato noodles," since they're made from potato starch, or "japchae noodles" after the dish they're commonly used to make. Dried work well for my purposes. Somyeon is similar to Japanese somen, and I use the thin wheat noodles interchangeably. They're available fresh or dried. Jjajangmyeon are chewy wheat noodles that you can buy dried or fresh. I find fresh Japanese ramen or even instant Korean ramyeon makes a fine substitute.

OKINAWAN PURPLE SWEET POTATOES

There are several kinds of purple sweet potatoes out there, but for the recipes in this book, I call for "Okinawan" sweet potatoes, also called "Hawaiian." They have beige skin, tapered ends, and pale purple flesh that deepens when they're cooked. The flesh is dense and super-starchy and the sweetness is subtle with a honeyed character. Look for them at Japanese markets, large Asian markets, markets that sell specialty produce, and online.

PERILLA LEAVES

Occasionally mislabeled "sesame leaves," the fresh jagged-edged green leaves (occasionally, with a purplish hue underneath) resemble Japanese shiso in appearance but only vaguely in flavor. Common in Korean cooking, they taste much bolder, with a similar minty, grassy vibe plus an element of anise as well. In this book, they're pickled (page 41), used as a finishing herb (page 108), and added to stews (page 103).

Find them at Korean markets, some catch-all Asian markets, and farmers markets.

ROASTED SEAWEED

For finishing all sorts of dishes, from hot soups to chilled noodles, I look to this store-bought product that's been brushed with oil, roasted until crisp, and seasoned with salt. Look for packages of full sheets at Korean markets or buy the snack packs sold at Asian markets and most supermarkets. Look for the simple salted kind or go rogue and use the wasabi flavor.

SAKE

I'm sober now, but you might enjoy drinking the slightly pricier bottles that have a subtle sweetness and floral, fruity qualities. However, for the purposes of cooking, I look to inexpensive, dry versions of this Japanese rice wine, though not anything labeled "cooking sake." You'll find it online, at Japanese markets, and at many wine stores.

SALT

I used Diamond Crystal brand kosher salt for developing the recipes in this book. Keep in mind that salt with finer crystals, such as Morton, will effectively add more salt per teaspoon than salt with larger crystals. In other words, if you're using Morton or fine sea salt, start with a little less than half the amount that the recipes call for and gradually adjust to taste.

SHIO KOJI

Also called white or creamy koji, this is a fermented mixture of water, salt, and a mold called koji kin (or *Aspergillus oryzae*), which is carefully cultivated on cooked grains like rice. The mold has a long history of application in Japanese cooking—it's used to make miso, sake, mirin, and soy sauce, or turned into this porridgelike ingredient. It tastes slightly sweet and smells a little funky and fruity, yet the magic comes when it's employed as a marinade or, as I do in this book, to add instant umami to quick kimchis.

It comes in other varieties, like brown and granulated, though the kind you're after here is white and creamy, and sold in either tubs or squeeze-y packs.

SHIO KOMBU

I often finish dishes with these shreds of kombu kelp that's been boiled in soy sauce then dried. They're salty and brimming with umami. My favorite brand, Matsumaeya, has especially thin shreds, but there are many brands out there, and you can always slice yours to your preference.

SHISO LEAVES

Not to be confused with perilla leaves, which share their serrated edges, fresh shiso leaves have a minty, citrusy astringency. They're most commonly used in Japanese cooking, so your best bet for finding them is at a market that specializes in Japanese ingredients.

SICHUAN PEPPERCORNS

For the recipes in this book, you can use either red or green Sichuan peppercorns, though be aware that green ones deliver even more of the numbing, citrus-peel quality. To make Sichuan peppercorn powder, which is best ground from the whole spice (no toasting necessary), use a mortar or spice grinder, then sift to remove any coarse bits. The spice grinder will smell like Sichuan peppercorns for a while, but it'll be worth it.

SICHUAN PEPPERCORN OIL

I've tried but never succeeded in making homemade oil infused with the floral flavor and mouth-numbing tingle of Sichuan peppercorns that rivals good store-bought versions. I use the Wufeng Lihong brand, but there are other solid brands out there as well, and price is often a good guide to quality. The oil can be made from green or red Sichuan peppercorns—both types work for my purposes.

SOYBEAN SPROUTS

There are two main types of bean sprouts available in the US—soybean and mung bean. In Korean cooking, soybean sprouts (or kongnamul) are more common, and you can tell the difference, in case labeling is no help, by the more bulbous yellow bean from which they sprout. I'm no stickler, though, so I'll happily use mung bean sprouts in a pinch, and you can, too.

SOY SAUCE

While many of the recipes in this book skew Korean, and the cuisine has its own roster of distinctive soy sauces, my recipes were developed using Japanese soy sauce (the gluten-free cook can use tamari), because it's the easiest to access and it's the soy sauce I've been using since I started cooking. That said, feel free to use any kind you have—

Korean, Thai, Chinese—but do note that they'll differ in flavor and saltiness, so you may need to adjust the seasonings accordingly.

The only exception: A few recipes call for Japanese white soy sauce, which has both lighter color and a particularly delicate flavor that the recipes really benefit from. It's more expensive than common soy sauce, but well worth the investment.

TOASTED SESAME OIL

Deep brown and often sold in small bottles, toasted sesame oil is pressed from toasted sesame seeds and shares their toasty, nutty flavor. Before using, give the oil a few minutes at room temperature, so it's easier to pour.

TOFU

Tofu is common enough nowadays to not require too much explanation. Firm tofu has firm texture and silken tofu has a silky one. Smoked tofu is also labeled as such, though I recommend buying it from a Chinese market, where it'll be super-firm and nice and smoky. Otherwise, tofu, as you probably know, is available at most supermarkets, though your options will often be better at markets with a focus on Asian ingredients.

New to some may be sundubu, which is even softer than silken and sold in tubular vac-packs to be snipped at one end and gently squeezed into the pot. "Sun" (sometimes written "soon") indicates the softness of the tofu (or *dubu* in Korean) and is typically reserved only for the tofu stew called sundubu-jjigae (see page 97). It's available in markets with a Korean focus.

TOT OR HIJIKI

Known as *tot* in Korean and *hijiki* in Japanese, this sea vegetable is typically sold dried and requires rehydration. It expands a lot during soaking, so use a bigger bowl than you might think you need. Look for tot or hijiki in Asian markets, health food stores, and online.

VEGAN BUTTER

Most vegans have a favorite product, but I recommend you try Violife Plant Butter, which I've found has a great buttery flavor without any of the off-tastes you find in some butter substitutes.

YELLOW PICKLED RADISH

Called *takuan* in Japanese and *danmuji* in Korean, these sweet, crunchy bright-yellow radish pickles are available in the refrigerated section of markets with a focus on Japanese and Korean ingredients. Drain and rinse briefly before using.

ACKNOWLEDGMENTS

There are many people to thank for supporting me throughout the years, specifically the years it took to make this book. We laughed together, we cried together, and we ate a lot of food together. Many of you lent your precious dishes, artwork, and props for the photoshoot which made the food (and me) feel truly at home. Putting this together was no small feat and I am grateful for the countless hours of thoughtful hard work that went into molding this book into something I am truly proud of.

For this I would like to thank Sara Hiromi; Mino Bowien; Youngmi Mayer; Amy Cakes; Mariko Makino; JJ Goode; Justin Hager; Kristine Reano-Hager; Will Sheldon; Sandy Liang; Kim Hastreiter; my dad, Jim, and Melinda; Scarr and Meagan Pimentel; Carly Mark; Jaden Dunbar; Sasha Melnychuk; Alex Petty; Michelle Guintu; Rae Ravich; Phil Wong; Hillary Taymour; Ama Torres; Chloe Wise; Colin Favre; Louis Shannon; Lele Saveri; Keir Kramlich; Geoff Rickly; Dylan Kraus; Rebekah Campbell; Nino Asaro + Partanna; Lauren Devine; Andrew Yang + Roy Yang; David Hardie; Rob Ontell; Anthony Myint; Yu Bo; Brandon Jew; Chad Robertson; Paolo Laboa; Jeong Kwan; Liz Prueitt; Daniel Halpern, Gabriella Doob + the Ecco team; Kim Witherspoon + the Inkwell Management team; Henry Hargreaves; Katlin Taosaka; Rana Duzyol; Josh Burgess; Evyta Soendoro; Nico Alonso; Leia Jospé; Kate Bolster-Houghton; Jean Kim; Esther Kim; Melli Yoon; 8-Ball Community; Jared Andrukanis + ZPZ; Duc Loi; Siam Market; Lung Shan; Hodo Soy; SOS Chefs' Adam & Atef; Coming Soon's Helena & Fabiana; SoulCycle NOHO crew; Anthony Bourdain; and Jim Walrod.

Thank you to the Mission restaurant staff—your continued hard work and dedication is inspiring.

I can't wait for what comes next!

INDEX

(Page references in *italics* refer to illustrations.)

HarperCollins books may be purchased for educational, business, or sales promotional use. For information, please email the Special Markets Department at SPsales@harpercollins.com.

Ecco® and HarperCollins® are trademarks of HarperCollins Publishers.

FIRST EDITION

DESIGNED BY RENATA DE OLIVEIRA

Photography by Henry Hargreaves
Prop styling by Katlin Taosaka
Recipe development & food styling by Mariko Makino
Photograph on page xiii courtesy of Jim Bowien
Photograph on page xv by www.pestochampionship.it
Photograph on page xvi by Leia Jospé
Photographs on pages xviii and xix courtesy of Zero Point Zero
Photograph on page 150 by Craig Lee

Library of Congress Cataloging-in-Publication Data has been applied for.

ISBN 978-0-06-301298-1

22 23 24 25 26   TC   10 9 8 7 6 5 4 3 2 1